The Chapel of
Trinity College
Oxford

The Chapel of Trinity College Oxford

1691–94

'A Beautifull Magnifficent Structure'

Martin Kemp

with an Appendix by
The Reverend Emma Percy

Photographs by
Tim Rawle

SCALA

First published in 2013 by
Scala Arts & Heritage Publishers Ltd
21 Queen Anne's Gate
London SW1H 9BU
www.scalapublishers.com

in association with
Trinity College
Broad Street
Oxford OX1 3BH

ISBN: 978-1-85759-824-7 (paperback)
ISBN: 978-1-85759-825-4 (hardback)

Principal photography by Tim Rawle
Designed by Isambard Thomas
Copy editor: Sarah Kane
Project manager: Oliver Craske
Index: Judd Flogdell

Printed in Turkey
10 9 8 7 6 5 4 3 2 1

Frontispiece: Detail of the panel in the screen,
viewed from the Chapel.

PREFACE

When, as the new Professor of the History of Art, I arrived at Trinity in September 1995, the Chapel was an immediate source of pleasure. It is one of those buildings that, in its architectural form and decoration, just feels 'right'. As a postgraduate at the Courtauld Institute of Art I had studied a course on British architecture of the later seventeenth and early eighteenth centuries with the late lamented Peter Murray, visiting almost all the City churches designed by Sir Christopher Wren. I had not traversed this territory since then, but good memories were stirred. Over the years I have looked hard at the Chapel many times. Its artful combination of apparently simple harmony and subtle complexity gradually revealed itself as I looked in different ways from various viewing positions in the interior, and as I asked different questions I became aware of its special position in British design of the period and how it continues to engage us today. What follows is a way of paying homage to those who worked on its realisation, most notably Ralph Bathurst, the President of the College who I am arguing was the 'author' of the scheme in all its aspects. It is also a thank-you to the College itself. As a professor of the central University, my relationship was different from that of the teaching Fellows, and I did little enough for Trinity while I was heavily occupied in transforming the Department of the History of Art into a larger entity, and in instituting the undergraduate degree. I am happy – now as an emeritus professor and honorary Fellow – to do something to repay my debt to what must be one of the most amenable and friendly colleges in the University.

I have also incurred significant debts in writing this study. The first and most indelible is to Clare Hopkins, the College Archivist. Her very fine history of the College, *Trinity: 450 Years of an Oxford College Community*, published in the anniversary year of 2005, provided the frame for my research. Indeed, the present book may be seen as an extended footnote to her history. She has also in person been unstinting in her support, sharing her knowledge throughout and assisting crucially with the transcription of documents. She is not responsible for any errors that may have crept in, but without her they would have been legion. I have received invaluable help from Jim Nottingham in understanding the two prints and surviving copper plates which provide key evidence for the evolution of the design.

The fine photographs of the Chapel have been taken by Tim Rawle, whose skills as an architectural photographer and keen appreciation of buildings and their decoration have raised this modest book into the realm of something visually special. Celia Bockmuehl was responsible for the excellent photographs of documents, drawings, prints and photographs held in the College Archives. Their photographic accomplishments have met with a matching response from Scala, most notably Oliver Craske, who has overseen all aspects of the book's format, editing and production with enthusiasm and exemplary good judgement. Isambard Thomas has designed the book in a way that responds deeply to the qualities of the Chapel as a visual experience. Sarah Kane has copy-edited the text with admirable care and attention.

Belinda Beaton, who was studying for a doctorate in the Department, enthusiastically conducted important research on all aspects of the Chapel and its context, assembling diverse bodies of published and unpublished material with great determination. We looked fruitfully at drawings and buildings together. The resources she provided have been constantly at my elbow during the writing of this study. Her work was facilitated by a grant from the College, without which nothing would have been achieved. Gaye Morgan greatly assisted our studies of the important collection of Wren drawings at All Souls and helped in obtaining images for this book.

Kevin Knott, the Estates Bursar, has been a great source of enthusiastic support throughout, both personally and on behalf of Trinity. Successive Chaplains Trevor Williams and Emma Percy have been unfailingly encouraging, as has Steve Griffiths, the Buildings Manager, who has facilitated the close study of the interior. Dr Stephen Harris, Druce Curator of the Oxford University Herbaria, kindly scrutinised the wood used in the Chapel by both surface inspection and the taking of samples, not least to confirm the use of Bermuda cedar. The whole enterprise has been overseen with wry good humour and unfailing interest by successive Presidents, the Hon. Michael Beloff QC and Sir Ivor Roberts. There must have been times when the project seemed to them to be based more on hope than expectation.

In spite of my tyro studies of British architecture many years ago, I very much cannot claim to be an expert in the subject. I have relied upon the ghost of the late Sir Howard Colvin, the undisputed authority on everything architectural in Oxford and far beyond. His *A Biographical Dictionary of British Architects* remains a seminal source. I hope he would not have been too critical of what this 'amateur' has done. He was after all deeply appreciative of amateur architects of the period. I have also gained much from the wisdom of Geoffrey Tyack, whose knowledge of Oxford architecture is encyclopaedic. More directly I have benefited greatly from the work and person of Anthony Geraghty, whose unravelling of the personalities in Wren's workshop has been crucial to my conclusions. I have also benefited from discussion of plasterwork with Victoria Vernier and Claire Gapper. David Esterly willingly shared his knowledge of Gibbons.

I am very pleased to be able include a study of the iconography of the current stained-glass windows by the Reverend Emma Percy, the College's Chaplain. The windows serve as a kind of theological commentary on the ancestry of the Chapel. The index has been completed by my excellent Personal Assistant, Judith (Judd) Flogdell, who has been a pillar of support throughout.

I have laid out the main text in three sections. The first, somewhat unusually, is envisaged as a visit to the Chapel in 1694, the year of its completion. This seems a good way to acknowledge the continuity of appearance in the Chapel and to bring out its extraordinary qualities without getting tangled up with questions of authorship. The second deals with the architectural history of the building and Bathurst's indomitable fundraising. We will also look at Wren's designs for the new residence, and the evidence of his engagement with the designs for the Chapel. The final part will examine the remarkable campaign of interior decoration, which has resulted in one of the most effective and integrated ensembles of painting and sculpture in any chapel in Britain.

I A SACRED THEATRE FOR THE SENSES

1. Interior of the Chapel, looking east.

There are several good Colleges I saw most of y^m … In Trinity Colledge is a fine neate Chapple, new made, finely painted … which was not ffinish'd the Last tyme I was at Oxford but now it is a Beautifull Magnifficent Structure. Its Lofty and Curiously painted – the Rooffe and Sides ye history of Christ's ascension a very ffine Carving of thin white wood just Like that at Windsor it being the same hand. The whole Chappel is Wanscoated with Walnut tree and the fine sweet wood ye same y^t ye Lord Orfford brought over when high admiral of England, and has wanscoated his hall and staircase with. It is sweet like Cedar and of a Reddish Coullr, but ye graine much ffiner and well vein'd.[1]

Our perceptive and appreciative witness is the remarkable Celia Fiennes, native of Salisbury, who journeyed – mainly side-saddle – across all the English counties over a span of almost twenty years from 1684. Celia described her initial reason as being a quest 'to regain my health by variety and change of aire and exercise'. This ostensible motive was extensively transformed over the years, and she became a uniquely dedicated witness to the visual character of English town and country, always with an eager eye on the spas and 'physic gardens' that might benefit her constitution. Not least, in a partisan spirit, she aspired to 'cure the evil Itch of overvalueing fforeign parts'. She seems to have completed the writing up of her journeys in 1702, but her accounts were not published until 1888. Celia visited Oxford for the second time in 1695, the Chapel at Trinity College having been finished little more than a year earlier. It was very much the latest thing to see in Oxford, and it was still the prime choice of Peter the Great of Russia when he visited the city privately in 1698.[2]

What these and other early witnesses encountered has for the most part changed to a remarkably limited degree over the years. We can in our mind's eye experience what a visitor in 1694 would have come across.

We are visiting a college that was being transformed under the seminal presidency of Ralph Bathurst, a notable man of letters, ordained in the Church of England and trained in medicine, who was deeply involved in the intellectual initiatives that had led to the forming of the Royal Society (fig. 2).[3] Amongst his friends was the mathematician, astronomer and architect Sir Christopher Wren. His three lectures on respiration had been so highly regarded that Robert Boyle had taken the manuscript to London in 1656 with a view to having them printed, but Bathurst's reluctance to publish scuppered the plan.[4] In spite of his lack of published works, Bathurst was elected a Fellow of the Royal Society in 1663. Ten years later he served as Vice-Chancellor of the University.

Entering from Broad Street through a Gothic entrance, known in a drawing by the Fellow and antiquarian Francis Wise (fig. 3), our 1694 visitor is presented with an ample and relaxed façade in the latest English classical manner. The wall that had run parallel to the boundary with Balliol, forming a lane wide enough for carriages from Broad Street to the arched entrance, had been moved to the right, opening up the vista. The wall is visible in the engraving by David Loggan (fig. 4), which also shows the old chapel before its demolition.

The new façade (fig. 5) comprises two main components. To the left is a three-storey tower, high enough to declare its presence, but essentially domestic in feel. It is neither military in its rhetoric nor assertively ecclesiastical in character. At its base is an open arch springing from simple capitals and framed by Ionic pilasters that support a plain cornice. Above this a double window is set within an arch and flanked by recessed panels and decorative cartouches at the centre of which are women's masks. The tympanum above the window proudly displays the sculpted

2. David Loggan, *Portrait of Ralph Bathurst*, engraving, 1694.

3. Francis Wise, *Gothic entrance from Broad Street*, pen-and-ink drawing, 1733.

4. David Loggan, 'Trinity College', from *Oxonia illustrata sive omnium celeberrimae istius universitatis collegiorum*, Oxford, 1675.

overleaf
5. Exterior of the Chapel, viewed from the south. The statue on the left (south-west) corner of the tower is Theology, and to the right is Mathematics.

Porta exterior antiqua Coll. Trinitatis Oxon.

COLLEGIUM St TRINITATIS

arms of the founder, Sir Thomas Pope: 'per pale or and azure on a chevron between three griffins' heads erased four fleurs-de-lys all counter-charged', amplified by two dragons' heads mounted on a wreath and with coronets around their neck. Around the shield active putti disport themselves, two blowing trumpets. The vertical frontispiece of the tower continues in the free upper storey with a single window and two broad lateral pilasters with recessed panels, which are adorned with cartouches of draperies, tassels and plant motifs hanging from rather basic lion masks. On either side of the pilasters are oddly complicated volutes that almost certainly play a minor structural role. The tower is topped by a balustrade that supports statues at its corners. We can see the personifications of Theology to the left and Mathematics to the right. Theology holds a book, while Mathematics holds geomet-rical compasses. They later became so heavily weathered that their attributes more or less disappeared over the centuries.

The façade as a whole terminates in quoins at either end, subtly underlining the fact we are dealing with a single building, not with a structure that has a separately attached tower. The main cornice that traverses the whole building breaks forward to mark the lower storeys of the tower, while the string course that marks the base of the main arched windows resumes its course to the left of the entrance at the base of the tower, again underscoring the unity of the whole. The façade to the right of the tower consists of four bays of windows, each immediately framed by slender bands and an arch with a keystone decorated with a head. Each bay is demarcated by a shallow Corinthian pilaster that stands sufficiently far from the margins of each window to provide a sense of ease rather than compression. As the balustrade above proceeds across the window bays, it is set slightly forward above each pilaster to form pedestals that support vases or urns from which flutter proud flames of gilded metal (fig. 6). The two closely paired urns to the right effectively punctuate the interval between the last pilaster and the quoins.

On the face of it, we might conceivably be looking at a library or dining hall, but anyone who knows what was happening in London will recognise the architectural vocabulary as that which Christopher Wren was establishing as the distinctive native language for his great set of City churches, during the

6. Flaming urns on the balustrade above the Chapel.

remarkable wave of building that followed the Great Fire of London in 1666. The harmonious ease of the Trinity design, with its judicious combination of geometrical articulation, classical elements, open surfaces and controlled clusters of carved decoration, seems at first sight to be entirely characteristic of Wren's architectural vocabulary. He was forging a style that allowed almost endless variations for each individual church, in ways that were highly inventive but always stopped short of flamboyance. Yet, when we look more carefully, Trinity Chapel somehow contrives not to look like the City churches, either individually or collectively. The tower is less towering; the combination of recessed panels with carved decorations is less than orthodox; the entrance arch is nowhere found in the London churches; and the relaxed composition of arched windows and pilasters does not appear in the fifty or so designs that emanated from Wren's office. The accent in which the language is spoken does not seem to be Sir Christopher's own. Why it looks so apparently Wrenian and yet decisively different will concern us later.

We pass through the entrance arch under the panelled ceiling of the passage through the tower and emerge into an almost square courtyard. In front and to the right are the old domestic ranges still retained from the earlier Durham College, with their dormer windows. The old college was established in the late thirteenth century to educate monks from St Cuthbert's in Durham, but its properties had been surrendered to the Crown during the Reformation, and it was subsequently made available to Thomas Pope.[5] To the left runs the old hall of Pope's foundation, some sixty feet long. The courtyard façade of the Chapel, as we turn to face it, presents a striking contrast in its modernity (fig. 7). Architecturally it is a mirror image of the street façade, with the notable exception that the end bay to the right is rather awkwardly overlapped by the end wall of the east range of the old building. The shield in the tympanum in this case displays the arms of Ralph Bathurst with his family motto, TIEN TA FOY – 'Keep thy Faith' or 'Hold Fast to Faith'.

Straining our gaze to the top of the tower, we note that the statues at the corners are identifiable as Medicine to the left and Astronomy to the right. Medicine holds a flask and a rod around which is coiled a snake, the symbol of healing associated with Asclepius. Astronomy carries the sphere of the heavens. We have already seen their counterparts, Theology and Mathematics, on the other side. We know that the Danish-born sculptor, Caius Gabriel Cibber, had earlier carved statues of Theology, Law, Medicine and Mathematics for the balustrade of Wren's library for Trinity College, Cambridge.[6] The Trinity quadrivium omits Law, which had not been included in the College's founding statutes. Medicine, also excluded from the statutes, is however present, presumably on the wishes of President Bathurst, who had switched from Theology to Medicine during the course of his studies. Perhaps Bathurst is making a statement about challenges to his presidency on the grounds that although he was ordained he had never become a Doctor of Divinity. The combined presence of Medicine and Astronomy on the courtyard side of the tower, which was then regarded as the prime view, is very much in keeping with the ideals of his intellectual circle.

Immediately to the left of the tower, we enter though a reasonably ample door that is strikingly devoid of rhetoric. We are in the shallow antechapel, flooded by light from tall windows to the south and north (fig. 8). A monumental and richly carved screen separates the space from the main body of the Chapel. The principal architectural elements have been constructed with impeccable skill from glowing walnut panels with architectural elements and carvings in Bermuda cedar, which has been stained darker for the decorative sculpting of the capitals of the fluted columns and the perforated panels of swirling vegetation on either side of the central doorway.

The so-called 'Bermuda cedar', actually a juniper, *Juniperus bermudiana*, is 'the fine sweet wood ye same yt ye Lord Orfford brought over when high admiral of England', of which Celia Fiennes spoke. The standard reading of her handwritten text gives the importer's name as Lord *Oxford*, but the reference is clearly to Edward Russell, 1st Earl of *Orford* and Admiral of the Fleet, whose house, Chippenham Park in Cambridgeshire, she described in 1698:

> The hall is very noble paved wth free stone, a squaire of black marble at Each Corner of ye freestone: there are two fine white marble tables veined wth bleu; its wanscoated wth wall nut tree, the pannells and Rims round wth mulbery tree y^t is a Lemon Coullour, and ye moldings beyond it round are of a sweete outlandish wood not much differing from Cedar but of a finer Graine, the Chaires are all the same.

The much-prized Bermuda cedar is renowned for its strength, lightness, colour and strongly aromatic odour. Celia was rightly struck by its sweetness of smell. By 1690 its export from Bermuda had long since been regulated in an attempt to conserve native stocks, and its use in Trinity and by Lord Orford is a sign of commitment to the finest woods that could be obtained.

9. The main body of the Chapel viewed through the entrance from the antechapel.

8. Entrance screen viewed from the antechapel.

10. The ceiling of the Chapel as viewed from the entrance screen, showing Pierre Berchet's *Christ in Glory* (oil on plaster). The rectangular panel below, featuring two angels bearing a cross, is above the altar (see page 22).

11. Grinling Gibbons's St Matthew, viewed from the antechapel.

12. Grinling Gibbons's St Mark.

(Identifying types of wood is far harder than is often assumed, not least by specialists in antique furniture. Stephen Harris, Druce Curator of the University Herbaria, inspected the woods and took samples to narrow down the possibilities. He confirms that the wood used for the carved decorations, including the figure sculpture, appears to be a *Juniperus* species, as is that for the free-standing architectural elements, at times stained and at other times not.)

This luscious wood seems to have been used in the five decorative urns atop the screen. At the centre of the pediment is an assertively ornamental shield. Heads of putti are placed in its upper corners, while grapes and ears of grain lower down refer to the wine and bread, symbolic of Christ's blood and flesh. Most spectacularly as we look upwards we become aware of two energetic figures of Evangelists swathed in dynamically angular draperies and that are leaning across the curves of the pediment. On the left is St Matthew with his angel and on the right St Mark with his lion (figs 11, 12). They both gaze heavenward towards the source of divine illumination, as yet undefined for us but apparent to them.

Passing through the central aperture in the screen, we enter the radiant space of the body of the Chapel (see fig. 1). As we look up immediately on entry, we become witnesses to the heavenly vision implied by the Evangelists' glances (fig. 10). Our view from this entry point is diagonally upwards into heaven, past two mighty angels, or rather archangels, who occupy a zone of celestial space lower than that into which Christ has already passed. Christ himself ascends in a blaze of golden glory, borne aloft on a cushion of clouds and flanked by ecstatically praying angels. His open arms, fluttering robes, divine expression and radiant aura of light rays indicate that his ascent is driven by spiritual rather than material forces. The ineffable realm of golden light, undefined in its form, is fringed by clusters of putti and cherubim. Passionate glances and emphatic gestures criss-cross the heavenly space.

There are three carefully differentiated ranks of angelic beings throughout the Chapel. Firstly there are the large angels adult in mien in the central painting. Then come the winged infants, complete in body, seen in the rectangular end panels and at the centre of each lateral wall. Finally there are the winged angelic heads. These three types should probably be identified with the biblical archangels, angels and cherubim.

Directly above, as we stand just within the threshold of the main space looking at the painting, a cheerful putto stares directly at us, smiling as he walks on air and waves palms in either hand. The palms refer to Christ's final entry into Jerusalem, when an enthusiastic crowd strewed his path with fronds. They are also symbols of the martyrs and of victory. We become aware that the background at the far and near ends of the space is characterised as blue sky, in contrast to the golden aperture through which Christ will pass. The ceiling is indeed 'finely painted', as Celia acknowledged.

As we step inside and look backwards and upwards (fig. 13) we encounter the highly active figures of St Luke with his ox and St John the Evangelist with his eagle, the counterparts to the two saints on the entrance side of the screen. All four Evangelists clutch the Gospels of which they were the authors. As before, one is bearded and the other clean-shaven, with clearly differentiated features, emphasising that they are human individuals. We notice that they are staring with urgent awe at Christ high above. Like the Saviour, they are supported in their elevated and potentially unstable locations by spiritual uplift rather than physical logic. The total effect of the painting and the sculpted figures is akin to that of the Transfiguration of Christ, in which three (not four) apostles on the summit of a mountain became witnesses to Christ's shining appearance in the sky. As we will see, the first thoughts about the ceiling painting adopted key characteristics of the Transfiguration.

The long painted panel at the west end of the ceiling, which had not made full sense when we were in the antechapel, now takes its full effect. Two angels gambol amongst clouds with instruments of the Passion (a hammer and nails, a spear, and a *flagellum*). They are painted in a way that is specifically orientated to our position standing just inside the screen. We now see that they are looking towards those who enter the antechapel.

We also notice two canopied thrones that are incorporated into the screen to the left and right of the entrance. That on the left (south) is for the President, while that on the right (north) is for the Vice-President. The perforated panels beside them are more richly carved than those on the outside screen and feature angels' heads in intimate communion (see the frontispiece).

As we turn and resume our progress into the Chapel, we become increasingly engaged by the second of the long rectangular painted panels, above the altar (fig. 10). Two counterpoised angels are bearing a diagonally disposed cross, with an apparent lack of effort not commensurate to its weight. The one to the left looks down towards the chamber in the left corner of the Chapel. The acronym INRI stands for 'Iesvs Nazarenvs Rex Iudaeorvm' (Jesus of Nazareth King of the Jews), decreed by Pilate to be inscribed mockingly on the cross. A putto to the right, who looks towards the glazed chamber below him, holds two further nails and the crown of thorns, close to a nail hole in the arms of the cross

13. Interior of the Chapel, looking west. The entrance screen is topped by St Luke and St John, carved by Grinling Gibbons. Either side of the entrance are canopied thrones. The ceiling panel above features Pierre Berchet's *Angels with Symbols of the Passion* (oil on plaster). The organ beyond is a nineteenth-century addition.

PSALMS

HYMNS
208
384
393
516

14. Rear choir stalls carved from oak.

15. Angels at the centre of the north wall.

16. Angels at the centre of the south wall.

overleaf
17. Interior of the Chapel, looking east.

from which blood is running. The physical nature of Christ's sacrifice is made fully evident.

To our left as we walk towards the altar between the choir stalls of fine oak (fig. 14) and across the complex tile pattern of the stone floor, we notice a pair of carved putti atop the raised cornice of the fine oak panelling at the centre of the left wall (fig. 15). As mirror images of each other, they stare divergently downwards at the entrance arch in the screen and at the altar. Their mouths are open as if they are reading out loud or singing from the open booklets that they hold. Between them is another finely wrought urn. Their companions on the other flank by contrast look intently with criss-cross glances to the Evangelists and the reredos above the altar (fig. 16). They confirm that the very space of the Chapel serves as a theatre for spiritual drama in which the alert and mobile spectator is an active participant.

As we walk past the mid-point the focus of our attention is drawn increasingly towards the east wall, which is articulated by a pair of detached columns supporting a cornice and curved pediment stepped back in the centre (fig. 17). The motif is similar to that on the outside and inside of the screen, but carried out on a notably more ample scale. This time the pediment supports a pair of large 'angels', powerfully winged, who are holding metal palms (figs 18, 19). Beside their elbows are crowns. Their rounded breasts, more than partly revealed, indicate that they are better identified as personifications of Victory rather than conventional Christian angels. Victory traditionally bears a palm and a wreath, here replaced by a crown. Alone of the beings in the main body of the Chapel, they address neither us nor the other sculpted or painted figures but look in an undefined way into space. Perhaps the intention is that they should do nothing to divert our attention too forcibly away from the altar and reredos.

In front of the altar is a balustrade with perforated panels. The framework is constructed from carved wooden blocks attached to a backing of pine (*Pinus* species) while the wooden blocks are juniper, that is to say almost certainly Bermuda cedar. Juniper is also used for the balusters, and in the perforated panels in the balustrade.

As we near the altar, we begin fully to appreciate the miraculous vitality of the limewood reredos and the wooden starburst framed at its centre. Around the rectangular frame, cherubim luxuriate in a bounty of fruit, flowers and vegetation, carved and undercut to awesome effect (fig. 20). This is virtuoso limewood carving of the very highest order. Sacramental grapes and grain are again evident amongst the array.

At first sight it looks as if symmetry rules. But within the shared profiles of the carved swags to the right and left, the motifs are orchestrated in counterpoint. Nowhere is this more evident than in the startlingly lifelike faces of the cherubim.

18. Victory on the left of the pediment.

19. Victory on the right of the pediment.

Some have their mouths open, apparently singing; others look on quietly; the lowest of them close their eyes in a mournful manner. The ideal is variety within unity. Wondering at the abundance of naturalistic motifs here and elsewhere in the decoration, we may recall that the central ideal of those who founded the Royal Society was to exploit intense observation and controlled experiment to reveal the organisational secrets of nature as a key to God's divine scheme of things. This was very much Bathurst's stance as a physician and theologian.

Within the frame above the altar, brilliantly inlaid walnut veneers of contrasting grain and colour mathematically describe an explosive burst of divine illumination (fig. 21). At the centre is a twelve-pointed star. The emission of light as starburst echoes the way that light rays emanate from Christ's head in the ceiling painting. Twelve is the number of hours in the day, months of the year, and disciples. Alternate rays, starting at the top, are given wavy contours, as was often the case with the sunburst of rays that emanate from the IHS monogram used by St Bernardino of Siena. Here the points of the second and fourth, the fifth and seventh, the eighth and tenth, and eleventh and first are linked by inlaid semicircles, and the whole is contained within a square. The intermediate intervals are linked by straight strips of inlay. The bands above and below the main square are formed from three smaller squares, the central ones of which contain an inscribed and rotated square with eight triangular insets. At the centre of the two rotated squares are eight-pointed stars. In the narrow, upright panels on either side of the central frame are horizontally compressed versions of the main motif in the central panel, above which are paired panels in inlaid wood. The effect of the central and two flanking fields is somewhat like a triptych. What appears at first sight to be a vacant space for a missing painting is actually full of interlocked geometry and implicit light that invites our contemplation. It is an expression of the intricate order of God's creation.

20. Detail of left drop of reredos, carved in limewood by Grinling Gibbons.

21. The inlaid starburst within the altar frame is in walnut veneer.

Geometry and the propagation of light were for the scientists of the Royal Society as perfect a manifestation of God's order as could be wished. We recall the statues of Mathematics and Astronomy on the tower. The expression of the final mystery of God as a mathematical abstraction confirms that the ultimate truth is not precisely realisable in terms of material reality or a graven image of God's person. We have seen that the painted heaven in the ceiling ultimately dissolves into a glare of formless luminescence.

The Chapel is dedicated to the Holy and Undivided Trinity, but Trinitarian imagery is implicit rather than explicit. Jesus is assertively present in the painted Glory on the ceiling, and the dove of the Holy Ghost is readily visible with the tools of the Passion in the elaborate plaster panel above the altar (fig. 22). The presence of God the Father is manifest as light and cosmic order, but nowhere is he represented in his conventional figurative guise.

The walnut veneering of the divine starburst is the high-point of the virtuoso panelling throughout the Chapel, in which the colour and graining of the wood is exploited for a subtle array of visual effects. The oak of the panelling behind the stalls is inlaid with notable intricacy, playing off varied grains and tints in a way that repays careful looking. Indeed, the way that the varied colours, tones and textures of the different woods react to different kinds of light and to the spectator's viewpoint plays a significant role in the Chapel's visual delight.

22. Plaster panel above the altar featuring the dove of the Holy Spirit, instruments of the Passion and the old chapel.

23. Decorative plaster panel on the ceiling, to the north side.

The plaster panel above the altar is of very high quality and replete with meaningful motifs. On either side of the radiant nimbus of clouds surrounding the asymmetrically placed dove of the Trinity are crosses, ladders, skull and bones appropriate for Golgotha, weapons including the spear that pierced Christ's side, two poles topped by sponges soaked in vinegar, his cloak, a jar of anointing oil, the sword with which St Peter was to sever a soldier's ear, the cock that was to crow when the saint later denied Christ, a crown of thorns, a scourge, some rope, and hammers, nails and pliers. The nature of Christ's sacrifice and suffering is again insistently underscored. In the background to the right of the nimbus we can see what may be a schematic image of the former Gothic chapel (consecrated in 1409), now of course no more.

The other plaster panels in the ceiling are densely filled with vegetal motifs and putti of no lesser quality than the exuberant limewood carvings (fig. 23). The names of the masterful plasterers are unknown, as is so often the case, but their skills in animating the compartments of the ceiling contribute integrally to the whole effect. It is likely that they worked in situ before the other painted and sculpted elements were completed. There is a frame of oak leaves around the main painting. Oak leaves are a notable feature of post-Restoration plasterwork, in recognition of the role played by the Boscobel oak in the escape of Charles II. This central display of loyalty to the Crown complements the proud array of royal arms in the plaster frieze.

The lateral panels contain skeins of twisted acanthus, luxuriant flowers and fruits, curvaceous palms and sinuous tendrils. The assortment is naturalistically decorative and punctuated by symbolic allusion, not least the grapes and ears of wheat. At the level below the frieze, large cartouches and swags endow the surfaces with elegant sculptural life in an essentially decorative manner. Running around the frieze itself is a series of shields separated by sprightly acanthus leaves. They contain a variety of royal and national heraldic devices, including those of Scotland, Wales and Ireland. On either side of the round badge directly above the altar are an animated lion wearing a crown and an alert unicorn with a coronet collar – the royal heraldic beasts. The badge itself is a variant of the star of the Order of the Garter, with emphatic rays of radiating light. Someone has taken a good deal of care to determine which motifs should be used and where they should most fittingly be placed.

In the corners to the left and right of the altar are two shallow compartments or alcoves, built in oak with walnut veneers and adorned with three urns and capitals in Bermuda cedar (fig. 24). We have already noted that these chambers attract the attention of two of the painted putti in the panel above. Through the glass windows of that on the left we glimpse two recumbent figures in alabaster (fig. 25). These are the founder of the College, Sir Thomas Pope, who died in 1559, and his wife – but which one? His first marriage had been annulled in 1536. In the same year he married the widowed Margaret Dormer, who herself died in 1539.

24. The alcove in the north-east corner of the Chapel containing the effigies of Sir Thomas Pope and his wife.

His third wife Elizabeth, also a widow, whom he married in 1541, was very active in securing Trinity's future after the founder's death, and it was she who arranged for the tomb to be made. Elizabeth herself was to remarry again, but never surrendered her commitment to her second husband's foundation. Thomas and Margaret had originally been interred in St Stephen's Walbrook in London but their bodies were transferred to Oxford at some time in the mid-1560s. Elizabeth on her death in 1593 was interred in the vault beside Sir Thomas. The recumbent effigies, carved in an accomplished manner with gilded details, are laid out in prayer, as was standard, and were presumably derived from those in St Stephen's. The founder himself is dressed as a knight, with his emblem of a griffin polychromed at his feet. It is not obvious whether the elaborately costumed woman is Margaret or Elizabeth, an ambiguity that might have been deliberate, though it is perhaps more probable that she is Elizabeth. At her feet is a small dog, the traditional emblem of fidelity. The dog is licking his mistress affectionately.

As viewed normally in its tightly fitting chamber the sides of the tomb are invisible, and Thomas's wife is difficult to see properly. But if sections of hinged panelling are opened the west and south faces become partially visible. The inscription on the frieze of the tomb mentions that the bodies of both Margaret and Elizabeth 'lie here' together with 'Thomas Pope, knight'. Panels with pigmented heraldic shields of Pope and his family run along the front face of the tomb's base, while the short, west end shows the husband and wife standing and holding scrolls and shields. The two other faces of the base of the tomb are not visible. Joseph Skelton's 1821 engravings in the *Antiquities of Trinity College* re-envisage the tomb as freed from its encasement (figs 26, 27). The equivalent oak compartment in the opposite corner of the Chapel is less deep and serves to allow female members of Presidents' families to witness the services. The main entrance for ladies is via a door in the east wall, but a door also opens into the Chapel itself.

The total effect is of a sacred theatre for the senses. We have the order of geometry in the rationale of the design, the reverent representation of nature in the wood carvings, the host of symbolic details, the great drama of Christ in Glory as witnessed by the Evangelists, the worshipful vitality of the various angels, the spacious light of the whole interior, the radiance of the painted ceiling and stars of inlaid wood, the sweet scent of the rich woods, the implicit voices of the choir of cherubim, the real music of the human choir and the organ, and the intonation of the preacher – all in the actual presence of the founder's mortal remains. Not the least of these sensory experiences is the scent that pervades the space, described by Thomas Warton, author of the 1748 biography of Bathurst: 'The work smells sweet, and carries the aroma of fragrant Lebanon.'[7]

28. J. W. Thomas, *Chapel from the Courtyard*, 1958. This photograph shows the poor state of the exterior stone before Norrington's restoration of 1959–62.

The whole Chapel is a remarkable essay in integrated form, effect, function and meaning; each part is thought through in the context of the whole. The design requires more than an ingenious architect, a clever painter and an accomplished sculptor working in concert. There must be a controlling intellect who understands the spiritual and functional integration of the all the many components in the Chapel's adornment. As a theologian and experimentalist, a master of the study of theological questions and of the investigation of man and nature, Ralph Bathurst is clearly recognisable as the author of the whole. Who actually worked on realising his vision in its whole and in its parts will concern us in the following chapters.

Having undertaken our imaginary 1694 visit, it will be worth pointing out the main ways in which our present experience differs, since changes have inevitably occurred.

On the exterior, the ravages of climate and more latterly acid rain have done their corrosive worst. By the 1950s the surface of the exterior stone of all the older

College buildings was in poor condition. The façades of the Chapel were heavily exfoliated and severely darkened (fig. 28). As part of a massive campaign of conservation undertaken during the presidency of Sir Arthur Norrington, the Chapel was largely resurfaced with Bath stone between 1959 and 1962. The effect is much as in the human body. The surface skin changes but the form remains the same. The female statues on the corners of the towers presented a different and insuperable problem, since they had been reduced to little more than eroded cores of their original selves, and their identifying attributes are now largely obscured. All that could be done was to consolidate them.

Passing to the interior, two notable changes are immediately apparent (fig. 29). On the right is a fine painting of the *Lamentation with Saints*, which is a good copy by Gaetano Canucci of the painting by Andrea del Sarto from *c.*1523 in the Palazzo Pitti in Florence. The copy was directly commissioned for the Chapel in 1870 by Nathaniel Nicholson, an alumnus of the College.[8] Above it is a strikingly grand organ case, carved in a manner that is generally compatible with the original decorations of the Chapel but actually erected in the last century. A photograph from a little after 1870 shows the open space on the west wall that would have allowed the Evangelists on the outside of the screen more adequate breathing space than they now enjoy (fig. 31). We can also see the Canucci painting in place. In the time of Bathurst any organ would have been smaller and not such an intrusive part of the Chapel's fixed furnishings. The photograph also shows the original plain glass of the windows.

The current stained glass dates from 1885–6 and was donated by Henry George Woods, the then Bursar. The windows, dedicated to seven saints, were designed in a 'Jacobethan' style by John William Brown of Newcastle, who was then working for the prolific firm of J.(James) B. Powell & Co. The history of the windows and the iconography of the saints is discussed by Emma Percy in the appendix. The style of the glass is not too much out of kilter with the design of the Chapel as a

29. Interior view, looking west, showing two additions: Canucci's 1870 painting and the later organ.

whole. And there are of course other modernisations, not least of the heating and lighting.

Some of the visual changes are subtle but significant. Overall the wood has acquired a darker patina, which for the most part is pleasing, but the starbursts of the altar panels are diminished in effect. It takes an effort of imagination to re-envisage the original energy of the design and the gleam of the inlaid walnut. The veneer has bent and buckled in places, and the ghosts of a series of cross bars are visible in certain lights, seemingly caused by a scaffold of battens behind the surface (fig. 30). The central starburst now only achieves something of its original effect when the sun enters at precisely the right angle to catch the centre of the array. The burst of golden light in the ceiling painting has also dimmed, not least as yellowed varnish has taken its toll, but here we can perhaps make the perceptual adjustment more readily. The effigies of Pope and his wife are now less brilliantly adorned by gilding and touches of colour than they once were.

With these caveats, we can nonetheless confirm that our visitor of 1694 returning now would see nothing that seriously compromises the original effect of the whole Chapel and its wonderfully orchestrated parts.

30. The cross bars behind the veneered walnut panel are visible when viewed at an oblique angle.

31. Anon. for Parkers Booksellers, *Interior of the Chapel looking west*, c.1870. Canucci's painting had just been mounted on the wall, but this was before the organ and stained glass were added.

2 RALPH BATHURST AND 'OUR WHOLE DESIGN'

On 4 December 1691 Ralph Bathurst wrote a letter to the 1st Earl of Craven (1608–1697) on both sides of a used envelope (figs 33, 34). The royalist and soldier William Craven, who had been a member of the College, prospered greatly during the Restoration. Bathurst had persuaded him to support his earlier building enterprises at Trinity and entertained hopes that the Earl would come good with a donation for the new project to rebuild the Chapel. The draft was as follows:

My L^d,

It is now about 26 yeares since I waited on your L^p at Drury house as also a little after at Clarendon house where the then Lord Chancellor was pleased to recommend to your L^p the errand I was at that time employed in. It was, humbly to crave some assistance toward an additionall Building then begun in our small College, which once had the honour to boast your L^p a member of it; & doth yet record your noble Beneficence to our Library. Your L^p then gave me hopes of some future favour from you, but Time and the want of opportunity, hath suffered it to languish untill now. It hath pleased God to adde many more happy years to your Life: and I yet at this time survive to solicite your L^{ps} charity, for the continuance and fulfilling of your kind purposes towards us. We are now engaged in the rebuilding of our chapell, and that whole south side of the college. It was always Homely enough, but of late growne very infirme and Ruinous, both in the Roofe and walls. I have strained my selfe to the utmost for raising the outward Bulke of it at my own charge: But there is still much behind, which our poore college is not able to finish without the assistance of such good friends as are willing to contribute to so pious a worke. It is a debt we think owing to such great and generous persons as your L^p to acquaint you with so faire an occasion of adding one more title to the Records of your worthy Actions; that you who have done so many noble things both Abroad long since, & all times in your owne city, may a little refresh the memory of your former Beneficence to our poor college, tho' otherwise nevere to be forgotten.

What we have done, and what we are yet to do, the Bearer Mr. Charlet (one of our senior Fellowes) can more particularly declare to your L^p; by whom also we humbly present a copy of our whole Designe; not doubting but your L^p will be pleased to favour

To yᵉ E. of Craven / Decemb 4. 1691.

My Lᵈ

It is now about 26 years since I waited on your Lᵖ at Drury house, & also a little after at Clarendon house, where the thᵉn Lᵈ Chancellor was pleased to recommend to your Lᵖ the errand I was at that time imploy'd in. It was, humbly to crave some assistance toward an additionall Building then begun in our small College, which once had the honour to boast your Lᵖ as a member of it; & doth yet record your noble Benefactio̅ to our Library. Your Lᵖ then gave me hopes of some future favour from you, but time & the want of Opportunity hath suffered it to languish untill now. It hath pleased God to adde many more happy years to your Life: and I yet surviving to solicite your Lᵖˢ charity at this time for the continuance of your kind purposes toward us. We are now engaged in rebuilding of our Chapell, and that whole South side of the College. It was always Homely enough, but of late grown very Infirme & Ruinous, both in the Roofe & Walls; I have strained my selfe to the utmost for raising the outward Bulke of it at my owne charge: But there is still much behind, which our poore College is not able to finish without the assistance of such good friends as are willing to contribute to so pious a worke.

What we have done, & what we are yet to do, the Bearer mr Chaskal (one of our Senior Fellowes) can now particularly declare to your Lᵖ; by whom also we humbly present a Copy of our whole Designe: not doubting but your Lᵖ will be pleased to favour it with your kind Influence; which our Society will ever be ready most thankfully to acknowledg, and more especially

your Honᵉˢ most humble & obed: serv. R. B.

*it with your kind influence; which our society will ever be ready most thankfully to
acknowledge, and more especially your Hon's most humble and obed. servt.*
RB
*We sent your L^p an account of our Library books as was desired, which we hope
came safe to your hands.*[9]

Bathurst confirmed in a draft of a letter to Nicholas Stratford, Bishop of Chester,
that it was specifically the interior of the Chapel that lay beyond his own purse.

My L^d,
*I doubt not but your L^p may already have heard of our last summers attempt for
rebuilding the South side of our college; always Homely* ['meane' written above]
*enough, but of late growne very infirme & Ruinous, especially in the Roofe of y^e
chapell and walls of the Treasury and Gate-house.*
The worthy Deane of Christ-church [Henry Aldrich], *and othere able judges in
Architecture, have thought it most advisable to begin our worke wholly upon new
Foundations; thereby to enlarge it both in Length & Breadth; and withall to make
it range bettere at each end, with the east & west sides of that Quadrangle.*
*The shell, or outward Bulke of all, (as the walls, Roofes, pinnacles, windowes, &c.)
I hope, by Gods blessing, to be able to finish at my own charge: but for the inward
furniture & ornamentall parts (as wainscott, seats, skreen, Altar-piece, marble,
seeling, Fretworke and the like) we must make bold to solicite the charity of such
good friends, as are able & willing to contribute to so pious a worke…*[10]

The letter to Craven is just one of a number of similar drafts in the College
archives, often addressed to alumni, and tailored to match each individual 'prospect'
(as they would now be called). The drafts, sometimes in whole or in part in Latin,
bear witness to Bathurst's testing of phrases that he thought might be appropriate
in each case. Any modern college president or development officer will readily
recognise the strategies being employed, not least the personal delivery of the
appeals to potentially major benefactors – in this case by a senior Fellow of the
College. A similar letter to John Sommers, the King's solicitor, explains that 'what
we have done and what we are yet to do the bearer Mr. Charlet, one of our senior
fellows can now particularly declare to you by whom we humbly present a printed
copy of our whole design'. Arthur Charlet (or Charlett) was then acting as Bursar
and was in the following year to be appointed Master of University College. His
father had earlier subscribed to Bathurst's fundraising for a new residence. The
engraving of 'our whole design' as presented to potential benefactors will concern
us in detail later.

There were, however, striking differences between this and a modern
fundraising campaign, leaving aside the President's facility in writing begging
letters in elegant Latin. Bathurst had explained that he was intending to finance the
shell of the building out of his own pocket, and each Fellow was expected to have
the means to be a significant subscriber on his own behalf. An undated draft to
Thomas Staynor pulls no punches.

You may remember that when you was admitted Fellow, you tooke an Oath to the
College omnibus consiliis – *mundo. Your hand-writing being now recovered, it is our*
earnest request that you would please in behalf of that society [next word illegible] of
ever you had received some considerable benefit whereof you was a member for many
yeares to write to Mr Laughores & Mr. Weston, or at least to dictate something that
may tend to our Benefit in this Exigence when we are faine to borrow many hundreds
to finish the great worke we have been forcd to undertake, unlesse we would venture our
lives every day under an Infirm & Ruinous Building. I have contributed my share for
finishing the outward Bulke as walls, Roofe and windowes &c more than I am well able:
For the Inward and ornamental partes, as the wainscot, seats, skreen, marble, fretworke
&c., we must be faine to solicit the [a blank space of ¾ of a line left here by RB] and
I am almost ashamed to tell you, that as yet we are more obliged to the gratitude of
many that have been servitors than to some that were sondre Fellowes & your owne
*Contemporaryes and such as have taken y*ᵉ *oath* de gratiis rependendis *which our*
statute requires of them: As for such as came into their Fellowships in irregular times
[during the Civil War] & otherwise thus the statute appoints. I thinke they are so
much the more obliged to make some recompence to the college, as they have received
the profits of it without performing the conditions. I know none that ever made this
evasion but only Mr Charles Sparkes, whom you may well remember, who was thrust
on our society in the late bad times: yet even He though over-wifed (not without some
remorse for his former omission) left us 30 £ at his death which we have now received.[11]

The appeal to the Earl of Craven did not fall on deaf ears. Henry Barker, then
Bursar, signed the receipt: 'Received from the Rt Noble Lord Craven by the hands
of the Reverend Mr. Bathurst, President of Trinity College, twenty pounds being a
gift to Trinity College Chapel in Oxford.'[12] A few responses to Bathurst's entreaties
met with pleas of poverty or infirmity. A particularly elaborate excuse comes from
Margaret Pratt, the widow of Sir George Pratt. George's cousin was Sir Roger
Pratt, the accomplished gentleman-architect who built Coleshill House for her.
Bathurst could be confident that she would appreciate the classicising style of the
projected Chapel. Her tardy answer was only sent in 1693.

Noble Sir,
*I am ashamed to say how long ago I received y*ʳ *letter in regard it has not bin answered*
*till now but I am sure it will turn y*ʳ *resentments into pity when y*ᵉ *shall know I have*
lain under a sever fitt of the Goute almost ever since which above other parts fell with
*y*ᵗ *violence upon my right hand untill within these 4 or 5 days I have not bin able ether*
to doe business or hold any correspondancy with my friends & twas not fit to represent
my Circomstances to you by another hand which I will with all truth and sincerity
informe you of with my own; my husband left me six thousand pounds in debt which
I could never clear of yet I have five grandchildren to doe for; I have parted with a
good share of my revenew to my eldest grandson; and paid three thousand pound to
*y*ᵉ *second the last year and am upon ye point to pay as much for my granddaughters*
*portion; besides I have many of my husbands relations & my own to keep. So y*ᵗ *god*
*knows I am struggling with necessity & in an utter incapacity to shew y*ᵗ *zeal my soule*

desires for the House of god and my respect
for y^r self who I have in ye highest esteem
for y^r many exalted excellencys: and y^e
Great obligations I have had to you; this
added to y^r goodness will I hope prevaile for
mercifull sentance upon her y^t will be failing
in anything y^t lyes in my power to serve you
under the character of
Your most affectionate friend and humble
servant
M Pratt[13]

Not to be discouraged, Bathurst replied:

Madam,
I had sooner returned my Thankes for the
Honour of your La^{ps} letter, had not the
Carryers Times been mistaken by my
servan. I am sorry to understand by it that
your L^p hath been so seriously handled with
That malady which is usually accounted the
Companion of the Rich: and that my letter
should have the Ill Fortune to come when
it was in your Right hand, which the
Scripture makes to be the Giving hand
['Matth 6.3' crossed out]. But since I find

35. Sir Christopher Wren, *First square plan of the new residence.*

it so well recovered to write with your wonted Accuratenesse, I hope it will also ere long
be able to extend it selfe toward the promoting of That pious worke which now humbly
craves your assistance. The many Thousands your La^p is pleased to mention yourself
engaged in, do but sharpen our Appetite, and increase our Hopes, that, though the
Feast goes another way, yet a small crum may possibly fall to us from so plentifull a
table. Five or ten pound will not be miss'd amongst such great summes; and yet will
make a welcome Addition to our slender stock; besides the Honour that will accrew to
us, when Present and Future Times shall find so worthy a name recorded amongst our
Benefactors. Whatever be the Event, yet your La^{ps} undeserved Favour to my self, and
affectionate Inclinations expressed towards the work we are now about shall ever with
the utmost Respect and Gratitude be acknowledged by
Hon^{ed} madam
your La^{ps}
most humble and faithfull servant.
R.B.
Oxon. Trin. Coll.
March 17 1693/4.[14]

The outcome of Bathurst's theologically informed entreaty is not recorded.

Wren and the new residence

The splendid scheme for the new Chapel, which had long been in the President's mind, was the culmination of a sustained campaign to transform Trinity's stock of deteriorated and dated buildings. Oxford college buildings had generally suffered during the Civil War, as a result of the University's resolute support of Charles I, and a number of chapels had fallen into a state of disrepair. For Bathurst the need to do something presented an opportunity to express Trinity's aspirations through a modern style of architecture.

The campaign had begun in 1665 with a much-needed new residence block for Gentlemen Commoners. The architect was Christopher Wren, who was then Savilian Professor of Astronomy at Oxford and was engaged in the building of the Sheldonian Theatre. Bathurst was one of the overseers of the accounts for the construction of the Sheldonian.

There is a plan by Wren in the College archives for a square building (fig. 35). It is labelled twice by Bathurst: 'Dr Wrens designe for building in the little Garden toward Balliol college 1665'; and 'Dr Wrens designe for Building in the little garden without the college gate 1664'. The costings are as follows: 'Stack of chimneyes 80 £; Stone walls 50 £; Flemish walls & roofe 250 £; Floores & Seiling 150 £; Partitions & doors 80 £; Windows & casements 70 £; Other Ironworke 30 £; Lead 25 £. The total is £735.' The design, with a protruding staircase, is for a structure only half the size of that built.[15] The reference to 'Flemish walls & roofe' denotes a gambrel roof that has two pitches, shallower above and steep below, as in the cross-section (see fig. 38).

Bathurst's and Wren's expanded ambitions are recorded in four drawings signed 'C. Wren' in the Wren collection at All Souls. Three are recognisably for the residence as built, with one that may show an earlier idea for it, a slight and tentative sketch for a four-storey structure (fig. 36).[16] The three measured and signed drawings show the plan of the ground floor, the attic storey with a gambrel roof and dormers, the front elevation and a cross-section (figs 37–39). The cross-section does not seem

36. Sir Christopher Wren, *Early sketch for the new residence (?).*

37. Sir Christopher Wren,
Elevation of the new residence.

38. Sir Christopher Wren,
Cross-section of the new residence.

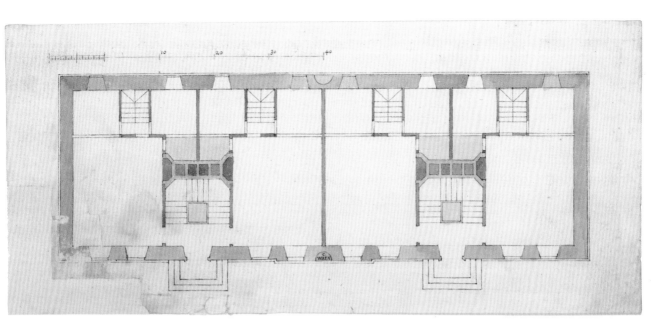

39. Sir Christopher Wren,
Ground floor plan of the new residence.

to correspond precisely with the plans and may relate to a variant scheme. All four are carefully executed in Wren's neat hand in pen and ink over pencil and shaded with grey wash. They show a simple, well-proportioned classical building, with lateral doors and a central bay emphasised by a triangular pediment below which is an arched niche.

The correspondence between Wren and Bathurst indicates that there was a lively debate about the best location for the new block, with at least two alternative designs. On 22 June 1665, Wren wrote a jokey but pointed letter to his friend (fig. 40):

> My hon^d Freind,
> I am confirmed (with Machiavell or some such unlucky fellow, 'tis noe matter whither I quote trew) that the world is generally governed by wordes. I perceive the name of a Quadrangle will carrie with it those you say may possibly be your Benefactors, though it be much the worse situation for the Chambers, and the Beauty of the Colledge and the Beauty of the particular pile of building, & If I had skill in enchantment to represent the pile first in one position then in another, that the difference might be evidently seen I should certainly make them of my opinion, or else I'le appeale to Monsieur Manzard, or Signior Bernini, both which I will see at Paris within this fortnight. But to be sober if any body as you say will pay for a Quadrangle there is noe dispute to be made let them have a Quadrangle though a lame one somewhat like a threelegged table. I sent last weeke to Minchin to give him a full account of the designe that was fitted for the grove. And if you resolve upon the other way of setting it in the Garden, you have two designes for that way alsoe, neither of which doe I know at present how to mend. I suppose the first of these 2 in the Books may please you best, to be set in the Garden; I meane the loose paper which contains a Ground plot only,

My hon.ᵈ freind.

        I am confirmed (with Machiavell
or some such unlucky fellow 'tis noe matter whither I
quote trew) that the world is governed by wordes. I per-
ceiue the Name of a Quadrangle will carrie it with those
you say may possibly be your Benefactors, though it be much
the worse situation for the Chambers, & the Beauty of the
Colledge. and the Beauty of the particular pile of building, & if
I had skill in enchantment to represent the pile. first in one
position then in another, that the difference might be euidently
seen I should certainly make them of my opinion, or else I'le appeale
to Monsieur Manzard or Signioo Bernini both wc.ʰ I shall see
at Paris within this fortnight. But to be sober if any body as
you say will pay for a Quadrangle there is noe. dispute to be
made let them haue a Quadrangle though a lame. one somwhat
like a threelegged table. I sent last weeke to Minchin to giue
him a full account of the designe that was fitted for the Groue
And if you resolue. upon the ~~last~~ other way of setting it in the
Garden, you haue 2 designes for that, neither of wc.ʰ doe I know
at present how to mend. I suppose. the first of those 2 ᴹᵗʰᵉ ᴮᵒᵒᵏˢ may please
you best, I meane. the loose paper wc.ʰ contains a groundplot on.y
with one bedroome & 2 studies to each Chamber, wc.ʰ Minchin cannot
be at a losse in, ~~in~~ this designe I intended the stories but 10 foot
high, & though I haue not particularly expressed an Upright for
that, I meant to haue used the same that is there glewed to the
other groundplot changing only the hight of the stories. If you
shew this part of the Leter to Minchin I know he will apprehend it

40. Letter from Sir Christopher Wren
to Ralph Bathurst, 22 June 1665.

*with one bedroome and 2 studies to each Chamber, which Minchin cannot be a losse in,
in this designe I intended the stories but 10 feet high: & though I have not particularly
expressed an Upright* [elevation] *for that, I meant to have used the same that is there
glewed to the other groundeplot, changing only the highth of the stories. If you shew
this part of the leter to Minchin I know he will apprehend it.*

*You need not use any apologies to me, for I must beg of you to beleeve you may
command me in thinges of greater moment, & that I love to serve you as your most
faithful and affectionate*

freind & servant,

Chr: Wren.[17]

Not the least interesting aspect of the letter is Wren's acknowledgement that
his skills in drawing were not sufficient to provide a scenographic presentation
of how his design would look in its preferred location. The 'Minchin' who was
charged with making sense of the alternative designs may be identified as Robert
Minchin, who had built the Bishop's Hostel at Trinity College, Cambridge in
1669–71. He had presumably been given responsibility by Wren for realising the
new residence. The books of designs for alternatives did not include those in All
Souls, since the drawings there are those that were originally retained in Wren's
workshop.

Notwithstanding his humorous name-dropping of the French architect Mansart
and the Italian sculptor and architect Bernini, Wren recognised that ultimately
those who pay the piper call the tune. One of the potential paymasters in this case
was Robert Skinner, Bishop of Worcester. In May 1665 Bathurst announced that
'we at first intended it in the Fellows' Garden, but for many reasons have transferred it to the upper part of the grove, where it will stand with much more beauty
and convenience'.[18] Seemingly he had been persuaded by Wren. However, Skinner
was not happy, and Bathurst back-tracked, writing on 2 July that 'we have now
in submission to your Lordship's wisdom and advice, transferred it back again to
the fellows garden, where we at first intended it, though much against the will of
some and the judgement of others, especially Dr Wren who is our chief designer'.[19]
The Bishop was in due course to donate £100, and no doubt encouraged others.[20]
The eventual cost was close to £1,500, almost twice that of the first square design.
The new building, standing in isolation to the north of the older quadrangle, can
be seen in the Loggan engraving (fig. 41), next to what remains of the fellows'
garden. The west limb of Wren's 'three-legged table' was realised when a second,
matching block was begun to the west. The elegantly pedimented blocks have since
been surmounted by a further storey, losing their pediments, very much to the
detriment of their appearance.

The written evidence for the Chapel

Wren was deeply involved in the architectural scheme for the new Chapel, but the
correspondence indicates that he was not the 'chief designer'. This becomes clear
if we look at the sequence of events revealed by the rather patchy surviving correspondence and related documentation. I intend to look at the principal documents

41. David Loggan, 'Trinity College', detail of fig. 4 (from *Oxonia illustrata sive omnium celeberrimae istius universitatis collegiorum*, 1675), showing the new residence.

in chronological order, noting the identities of the key people involved as far as is possible, and then to see what can reasonably be said about who was responsible for the design of the building.

Our first definite notice that the project was underway comes from 13 May 1691 when William Long of Ham wrote ponderously about his obtaining of timber, presumably in expectation that he would be awarded the contract for the work.

> *Sir*
>
> *Mr President*
>
> *I Am informed that your wor^{pp} doth desine to Repare the Colledge Chapell this yeare, and I doe hope that your wor^{pp} will be soe kinde to me as not to pute me oute of your faver and Louse the doeing of it for I doe Asuer you that when the thimber wase bought for it I tooke A great deale of paynes in the getting of it home for which I did not account anything for it to ye Colledge and all in hopes y^t I should have had ye manedgeing of it when it was used therefore I would umbly intreat your worship in my [next word obscured by the paste-down of a tear in the paper] not to imploy another workeman: for if that be the reson I do Asure your worshipp that of the too I will louse my countrys Business than your worshipps and that there shall be now man Doe your business better than my selfe, and I shall for ever Honour and Accknowleg your worshipp as my Greatess frind and there is now Man that shall serve you with greater fidelity in what in me lyes by being both true and faith to you and ye Colledge and industrious in what I undertacke then Sir your wor^{sppfull} moust Dutiful servant for ever to Command.*
>
> *Ham 13th May 1691 William Long.*[21]

By August the work was proceeding apace: the old chapel had been demolished and the shell of the new Chapel was rising. We learn this in a letter from Thomas Sykes of 10 August, which also speaks of a wooden model:

Sir,

I presume you may desire at this time more especially to hear from your College, which you are enlarging and adorning at your owne charg and therefore I hope will easily pardon me for the trouble I now give you.

The next day after you parted hence, Mr Almont and I was with one Kemster, to whom we shewd ye model of our Chappel, and took what advice he could give concerning it, but upon farther discourse with him concerning his undertaking ye masons work of it, he demanded near as much more as Piesly had offerd you to do it for, before you left us, and therefore we were utterly deterrd from coming to any Bargaine with him, and which was somthing worse he shewd us a letter he received from ye minister of Burford, requiring his coming hither, so that we could not gett rid of him without a Gratuity for his journey hither, of which you shall have a particular Account at your Returne. All that we could do therefore was to clapp upp a Bargaine with Piesly as soon as we could and upon ye Best Terms we could gett, lest after he had conferrd with Kemster as he did ye next day he should raise his Price upon us: I heartily wish this might please you at your Returne: All ye old Building is in a manner downe, and the New advanced farther then you can easily imagine, but as the work rises so proportionably ye mony left in my handes decreases. I hope Mr Phipps will provide what is necessary that it may not be at a stand hereafter before your Returne. As to news the small Pox continues still much in this place, and Dr Oborne of our College is lately fallen, but like to do well. Dr. Rudstone of St. John College dyed last weeke of a feaver, and ye Proctor of Balliol Coll: of ye same disease a little before him. This day one Mr. Lugg of that college succeeds in his place. I hope you gott well to your journeys end that you may continue so, and safely Returne is the hearty prayer of S^r, your most obliged & very humble servt.

Tho: Sykes.[22]

Sykes is a notable figure in Trinity's history. He entered as a humble 'servitor' in 1660, but such was his promise that he became a Fellow in 1667 and rose to the position of Lady Margaret Professor of Divinity in 1691. He was briefly to succeed Bathurst as President in 1704. We may find it strange that Bathurst was absent from College at such a crucial point until we realise that he was also Dean of Wells Cathedral, a post that brought with it substantial commitments. His enforced absences became something of a bone of contention in the College.

'Mr Phipps' is hard to identify. He was clearly playing an important role in the administration of the project, not least financially. It is possible that he was Francis Phippes, born in Oxford in 1629 and a graduate of Oriel.

Sykes's letter also speaks of Bartholomew Peisley, who was central to the project throughout. Peisley (1654–1715) was second in a dynasty of Oxford mason-architects. His father, who died in 1692, had been the mason for the chapel in St Edmund Hall, where Arthur Frogley undertook the splendid woodwork. The senior Peisley was also responsible for the senior common room at St John's.[23] The younger Peisley worked on the palace of Blenheim, constructing the span of the great bridge, and seemingly had a finger in many of Oxford's architectural pies.

overleaf
42. Candlelit service in the Chapel, 2012.

The Chancellor's accounts record that he has 'severall times been chief contriver of buildings of about £200 and £300 value'.[24]

The 'Kemster' who proved to be so much more expensive than Peisley was Christopher Kempster, who served as master mason on at least three of Wren's City Churches and at St Paul's, and had been recommended by Wren to take responsibility for Tom Tower at Christ Church. His main independent building was the handsome Town Hall in Abingdon.[25]

On 3 September Sykes wrote again to Bathurst, his letter revealing that there were problems with cash flow:

Honoured S^r,

Since my last I have had the favour of three letters from you, and in that sent by Mr Long, I received the 25 guineys mentioned: I have hitherto expected his Returne, otherwise you had sooner received an Answer, with my acknowledgements for these and all other kindnesses.

I am not able to inform you S^r what the good work you have been pleased to undertake will come to; And I verily beleive that Piesly himself cannot give a true estimate of it, but Mr. Almont and I agreed with him for nine shillings and six pence the Perch or Pole to be measured on such a manner as is most usual, and as we beleive will be to your advantage: He is by his bargaine to allow you as part of payment for his work, for all payd to him or otherwise layd out by you before this bargaine, excepting for stone, lime, and other materials, which are to be provided at your charg.

I have discoursd Mr. Phipps, concerning what mony may be wanting before your Returne: He tells me, that if what we have will not hold out, and you have no conveiniency of Returning, or sending any more, he will be sure to take care for what shall be necessary; and I presume there will be no want if you can be here about Michaelmas: But Reynolds ye carryer has not dealt fairly with you: On ye first of August, when he ought to have paid me 30£ according to ye note left in my hands, he could pay me but 15. Since that, he has been here againe, and promisd that he would certainly pay the Remainder before he left ye towne, but broak his word with me; I hope to gett it of him at his next Returne, which will be on Saturday, Septem: 12. I desire the return of my humble service to all my Friends, who are so kind as to Remember me, more particularly to Mr Layng, I am much obliged to them for their kindness b [obscured by the way the letter is pasted down] to none, so much as to you S^r for all your favours to
S^r
your most obliged & very humble servant,
Tho: Sykes

Trin: Coll: Oxon' Sept: 3^d. 91.

Our Society give their service to you S^r and are very sensible of your kindness to us. The small Pox continues and a young Commoner one D'Assigney is now sick of them in our College.[26]

The 'perch' or 'pole' was a rather variable measure, but was generally about 15–16 feet. Peisley was clearly experiencing difficulty in working out an overall cost for all the work he was expected to undertake at Trinity and was to be paid on a rolling basis. We have clear testimony from June 1691 of Peisley's close involvement at this time in the construction of the Chapel. Anthony Wood, the Oxford historian and antiquarian, was shown badly deteriorated coffins in the vault under the old chapel by 'Mr Piesley [sic] the master mason'.[27]

Sykes's next letter contains happier financial news:

> Rev*d* S*r*
> Your Letter with the Bill &c inclosed came safe to my handes, And Mr Hutchins hath paid the 100 li according to Mr Hole's order. This day John Reynolds also paid me 15 li of the Remander of the 30 li you Lent him, And Mr. Phips tells me that he shall very suddainly receive more mony upon your Account, so that I hope we shall not only discharg all due from you for the Chapel, but have a good fund in our handes at your Returne.
> I shall not undertake to acquaint you how the work goes on, Mr Beacham (who does me the favour to convey this to you) can more fully relate what progress is made in it, then I can write: It Remaines onely that I heartily wish and pray for your good health, and as soon as your affaires will permity y*r* safe Returne, assuring you that you will be most welcome to our whole Society, & more especially to,
> Hon'd sr
> Your very obliged and humble serv't
> Tho: Sykes
> My very humble service pray S*r* to all Friends
> 14 September 1691[28]

The costs of this phase of summer building were thus underwritten by Bathurst himself. In the winter, as building work slowed, the President embarked on the fundraising campaign for the interior, composing his begging letters to the Earl of Craven and others, as we have seen.

On 25 February 1692, in anticipation of better weather for building, we first learn of Wren's involvement with the design. The tone of Bathurst's letter conveys a sense of urgency.

> Worthy S*r*
> When I sent Mr Phips to wait on you with a scheme of [next word crossed out] new Building, he tolled me how kindly you was pleased to express your remembrance of me: & that you would send me your thoughts concerning our Designe; & particularly of the Pinnacles, which as they were superadded to our first Draught, so, I must confesse I would be well content to have omitted with your Approbation. The season for our falling to work again will now speedily coming on, which makes me the more hasten to entreat from you y*e* trouble of 2 or 3 lines in relation to y*e* Presents whereby you will farther oblige S*r* your old freind & ever faithfull servt.[29]

On 2 March Wren expeditiously replied:

Sir,

I am extremely glad to hear of your good health, and, what is more, that you are vigorous and active, and employed in building. I considered the designe you sent me of your chapel, which in the main is very well, and believe your work is too far advanced to admit of any advice: however, I have sent my thoughts which will be of use to the mason to form his mouldings.

He will find two sorts of cornice; he may use either. I did not well comprehend how the tower would have good bearing upon that side where the stairs rise. I have ventured upon a change of the staire, to leave the wall next the porch of sufficient scantling [beams] to beare that part which rises above the roofes adjoining. There is no necessity for pinnacles; and those expressed in the printed design are much too slender. I have given another way to the rayle and balluster, which will admit of a vase that will stand properly above the pilaster.

Sir, I wish you success, and health, and long life, with all the affection that is due from Your obliged, faithful friend and humble servant,
Chr Wren
P.S. A little deal box, with a drawing in it, is sent by Thomas Moore, Oxford carrier.[30]

Subsequent documentation confirms the continued vigour of Bathurst's fund-raising, even as the Chapel neared completion. In March 1694, Bathurst received a letter from Samuel du Gard, a Fellow who became Rector of Forton. He speaks of a donation from R. Unton (perhaps a descendant of Sir Henry Unton of Wadley Manor, Faringdon):

…Mr Untons Circumstances (which are much lower than I thought them,) make his 5 £ from his good will, to be, in some sort, equal to a larger summe. And, Sir, would you please, in one line to him, to signify your kind acceptance of it, I am persuaded it would be a great cheering to his old age. I am heartily glad to hear how worthily your Chapell is spoken of; and how for Strength and Beauty it is reckond among the Chief Ornaments of the university…[31]

The Chapel was complete by 27 March 1694, when Bathurst contacted the Bishop of Winchester about its consecration. He informed the Bishop that 'our new chapel hath prospered so well as that (with the help of what Other good friends have Given or Lent to us) the work is now brought to a handsome perfection'.[32] He requests that the Bishop of Oxford be asked to lead the ceremony: 'We cannot be so bold as to invite your Lord to so great a trouble; but rather entreat that being our Visitor and Patron, you would be pleased to signify in a few lines your pleasure & confess that His Ld Bishop of Oxford … may perform this pious office in your stead, which we find his Lord very ready to do'. Four days later the Bishop of Winchester readily assented to Bathurst's plan.[33] Accordingly, on 12 April 1694, the Bishop of Oxford, John Hough, oversaw the consecration. Thomas Sykes delivered the inaugural sermon, which was subsequently published with an effusive dedicatory letter to Bathurst. To complete such a structure with its elaborate interior in under three years was a considerable achievement.

The known documentation contains only scant details of who was paid for doing what between 1691 and 1694. We have no bursarial accounts during the main phase of the work to tell us who was in charge of the architectural design, who executed the carvings and who created the paintings. However, we are better informed about the execution of the joinery and stonework. Settlements of account and bonds for maintenance help fill out that part of the picture.

In 1691 Arthur Frogley, the architectural joiner, was paid a fee of £230.[34] He had ten years earlier been responsible for the sophisticated panelling of 'Flanders oak' in the Common Room (now the Old Bursary), towards which College members had subscribed £54.[35] On 24 May 1694, after completion, Frogley signed a receipt indicating that he had in total been paid the large sum of £1,140 for his work on the joinery of the Chapel:

> *Know all men by these presents that I Arthur ffrogley of the City of Oxford Joyner have had and received the day of the date hereof of the Rever[d] Mr Michael Harding Bursar of Trinitie Coll: in the University of Oxon the summe of One Hundred and Ninety Pounds of lawfull money of England part of One Thousand One Hundred and fforty Pounds being full paym[t] for all the Joyners work done in the new erected Chappel of the sd coll: by me the sd Arthur ffrogley and I the sd Arthur do by those presents for me, my heires, Exe[rs] and Admini[rs] remise release and forever quitt claime unto the said Michael Harding as also unto the said Presid[t] ffellows and schollars and their successors All & all manner of Action and Actions cause and causes of Accon', debts dues accounts summe and sums of money and demands whatsoever from the beginning of the world to the day of the date hereof in witness whereof I have hereunto sett my hand and seale the foure and twentieth day of May in the sixth yeaer of their ma[ties] reignes, annoque domini 1694.[36]*

On 9 November 1693 Frogley deposited a bond of £100 to guarantee that he would 'during the space of ten whole years commencing from the date hereof well and workman-like repair, maintain, and keep all the said joiners work'.[37] Frogley, who as previously mentioned undertook the woodwork in the Common Room, worked widely on projects across the University, including the Sheldonian, and was often associated with Peisley, whom we have already encountered as the master mason.

On the same day Peisley himself contracted to pave the floor with 'the best black and white Italian marble … according to the printed design'.[38] Peisley signed his bond of £20 to ensure that he would 'repair … the marble pavement by him the said Bartholomew to be laid in the inner chapel of Trinity College aforesaid lately built for and during the time of ten years from and after the finishing of the same Pavement'.[39]

Three designs

In the absence of direct written testimony about the authorship of the master-design for the whole and parts of the Chapel, we need to turn to the visual evidence. In the next chapter we will look at the painting and sculpture. For the moment we will concentrate on the architecture and fixtures of the exterior and interior.

Fortunately the engraved design that was sent out to potential benefactors in winter 1691 is known at present in one surviving copy (fig. 43). It is in the Christ Church collection of Henry Aldrich, whom we know was consulted about the design. The print is impressively large. Given its function, as an illustration to accompany the begging letters, there may have been a small print run. It is by Michael Burghers, the Dutch engraver, and is entitled *The Orthography* [Elevation] *and Ichnography* [Plan] *of Trinity College Chappel in Oxford*, dated 1691 and signed 'M Burghers sculp[sit]'. A skilled draftsman and meticulous engraver, Burghers became a resident of Oxford. He enjoyed a long association with the University Press and played an important role in recording University and college buildings. His first engraving of Trinity records the design *before* the intervention of Wren and is the prime evidence for any attribution of the original scheme. The elevation of the exterior is shown from the quadrangle side, which was clearly considered the more important elevation at this time. It differs in a number of important respects from the Chapel as built.

It exhibits different fenestration on the two upper floors of the tower, which is topped by slender pinnacles. The two sets of paired windows with swags and inset panels are rather old-fashioned. There is no provision for a shield on the first floor, but there is an indication of one above the door to the interior. The balustrade also carries the pinnacles decried by Wren, and is oddly articulated in relation to the pilasters below. Normally the balustrade above each pilaster would be marked by an emphatic feature such as a pedestal rather than a long recessed panel. The articulation of the pilasters and arched windows also differs significantly. In the engraved design, the pilasters are set against piers, with the arches of the windows springing from the cornice of the piers. Although the piers are wider than usual, this is the standard 'coliseum' elevation and was very common. It appears in more canonical form in Wren's library for Trinity College, Cambridge. As built, the arches of the Chapel windows spring from capitals at the top of the narrow bands (rather than pilasters) at the side of each window. The difference may seem slight, but it is crucial to the grammar of the design. We are not dealing with a series of piers with attached pilasters between which are arched windows but with a *wall surface* that is perforated by arched windows and articulated by pilasters. The *concept* is essentially different. It is strange that the more customary piers-and-columns concept characterises all the drawn and printed designs, as we will see.

Passing to the interior in the engraving, we see that the pediment of the screen carries figures of angels or Victories rather than Evangelists. There are no putti on the raised cornice in the centre of the lateral panels, and the corner chambers are equipped with curtains. The architecture and decoration of the altar wall is less grand in scale, with no sign of elaborate carving other than two further angels or

43. Michael Burghers, *The Orthography and Ichnography of Trinity College Chappel in Oxford*, first version, 1691.

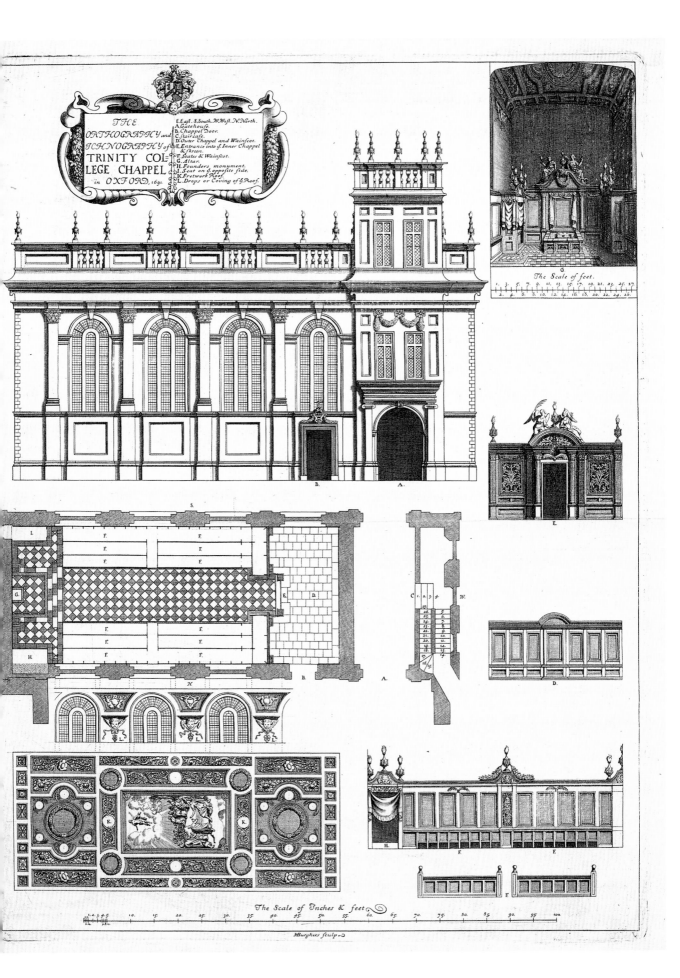

THE
ORTHOGRAPHY and
ICHNOGRAPHY of
TRINITY COL-
LEGE CHAPPEL
in OXFORD, 1691.

E. E.aſt. S.South. W.Weſt. N.North.
A. Gatehouſe.
B. Chappel Door.
C. Staircaſe.
D. Outer Chappel and Wainſcot.
E. Entrance into ẏ Inner Chappel & Skreen.
F. Seates & Wainſcot.
G. Altar.
H. Founders monument.
I. Seat on ẏ oppoſite ſide.
K. Fretwork Roof.
L. Drops or Coving of ẏ Roof.

The Scale of feet.

The Scale of Inches & feet.

M.Burghers ſculp.

Victories on the pediment. The ceiling is partitioned to provide a main rectangular field for a projected painting of the *Ascension*, which would actually be orientated the wrong way for the spectator entering the Chapel (see figs 47, 48). The iconography seems to blend the conventional Ascension with the Transfiguration, since, like the latter, it takes place around the summit of a hill or mountain and Christ is characterised as a source of intense light. It lacks the illusionism that was Berchet's speciality, suggesting that he was not involved at this stage. The floor at this stage is laid in a simple alternating pattern, diagonally orientated.

The overall impression of the design is that it is a pleasing if not always idiomatic exploitation of Wren's architectural language. It has been suggested that Henry Aldrich, Dean of Christ Church, who is known as an architect, was responsible. A classicist, logician, mathematician, musician and able draftsman, the polymathic Aldrich planned a treatise on architecture, the first parts of which were published as *Elementa architecturae civilis ad Vitruvii veterumque disciplinam; et recentiorum praesertim a Paladii exempla probatiora concinnata* in 1710, the year of his death.[40] However, Bathurst mentions Aldrich only in connection with general consultation about the Chapel, naming him amongst those from whom he sought advice. If Aldrich had been the guiding hand in the design sent for Wren's comments, one would have expected Bathurst to mention it. Aldrich's taste was for a more dogmatic classicism, founded on Vitruvius and Palladio, as proclaimed in the full title and illustrations of his book. His Peckwater Quadrangle in Christ Church aspires to a Palladian orthodoxy of a quite different cast from the more relaxed grammar of Trinity Chapel.

Aldrich's presence as an adviser does serve to remind us that the years following the Restoration were, *par excellence*, the age of the 'amateur' architect.[41] Wren himself began as an 'amateur', and Roger Pratt, gentleman-architect of Coleshill, never worked as a professional practitioner. It became unexceptional for educated and learned men, including ordained ministers, to turn their hands to a bit of architectural design. A basic knowledge of the classical vocabulary and a decent ability to draw with straight-edge and compass provided the necessary foundations. As in France, we often find those who have accomplishments in the precise sciences and medicine turning to architecture, as did Wren and Hooke in England. Bathurst fits this profile well. I think it is worth considering that his description of what appears in the 1691 engraving as 'our whole design' should be taken rather literally. He may be considered as the 'author' of the design, not so much in the modern sense as a sole genius-architect, but as the shaping intelligence at the head of a team of people who could contribute to different facets of the scheme. Such a situation was very common during this and earlier periods.

The well-connected and alert Bathurst knew precisely what was required for a modern chapel that would suit Trinity's particular needs in terms of form and content. Bathurst with Bartholomew Peisley, the experienced mason-architect, and Arthur Frogley, the architectural joiner, would have been capable of originating the basic elements of the design in the engraving. In this scenario, Peisley would have been the actual draftsman of the working drawings and Frogley the maker of the wooden model, while Burghers used his graphic skills to describe the project for benefactors. Perhaps it was the engraver who sketched in the idea for the *Ascension* and the statuary on Bathurst's instructions. The pleasing intelligence and ungrammatical idiosyncrasies of the design are consistent with such a compound process of conception.

The main argument against this thesis is that Peisley had not apparently been confirmed as the mason who would construct the Chapel in August 1691, when the wooden model was shown to Kempster so that he could quote for the work. However, Sykes was clearly interested in getting the keenest price on Bathurst's account, and Peisley's involvement with the President at the design and planning stage might well not have carried a guarantee that he would undertake the actual building. In any event, Peisley would have been well placed to make a competitive tender to be confirmed as the master mason, as indeed happened.

The next design involves Wren's modifications in early spring 1692. The somewhat confusing account in Wren's letter can be clarified to a large extent by an elevation drawing among the Wren papers at All Souls (fig. 44).[42] It has generally been assumed that this was the drawing contained in the 'little deal box' sent to Trinity. However, the presence of the drawing in the All Souls collection suggests strongly that this design never left Wren's office. Also it is clear that the drawing is by Nicholas Hawksmoor, who played such a leading and creative role amongst Wren's draftsmen. Hawksmoor's hand is firmer, more assertive and more impulsive in the details than Wren's. There is no mistaking it. The wriggling pen strokes that describe the capitals of the pilasters and the deft curls of dark ink that model the balusters are altogether characteristic. It may well be that the 'problem' of

44. Nicholas Hawksmoor, Design for the courtyard façade of the Chapel.

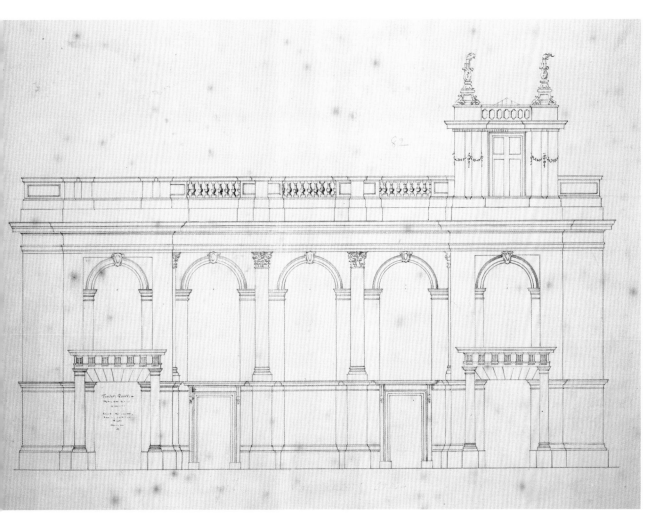

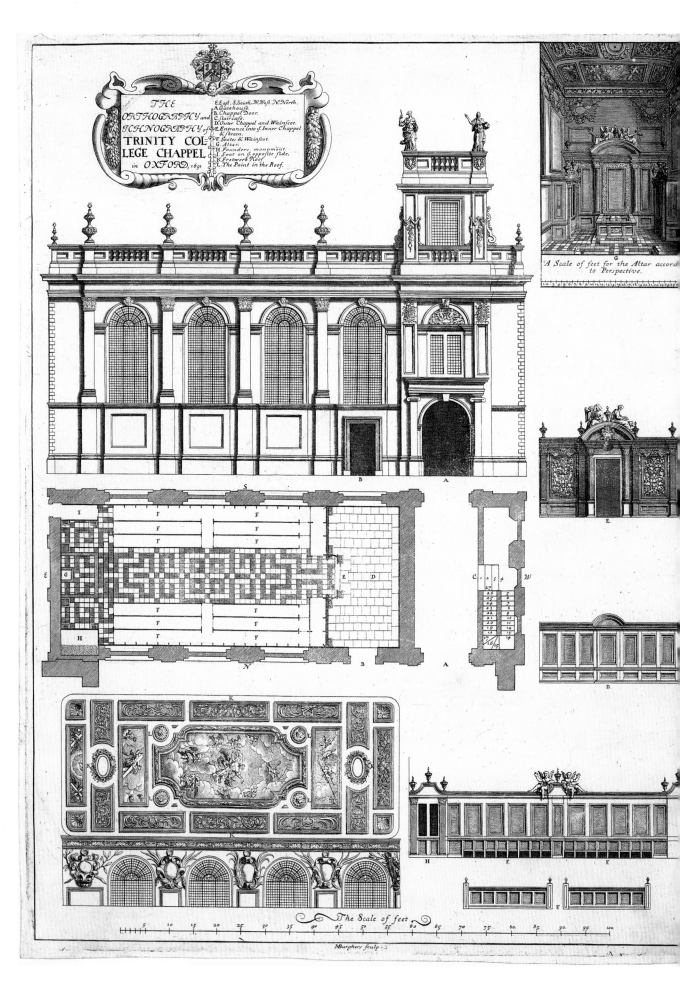

THE
ORTHOGRAPHY and
ICHNOGRAPHY of
TRINITY COL-
LEGE CHAPPEL
in OXFORD, 1691.

E. East. S. South. W. West. N. North.
A. Gatehouse.
B. Chappel Door.
C. Staircase.
D. Outer Chappel and Wainscot.
E. Entrance into ʃ. Inner Chappel & ʃcreen.
F. Seates & Wainscot.
G. Altar.
H. Founders monument.
I. Seat on ʃ. opposite ʃide.
K. Fretwork Roof.
L. The Paint in the Roof.

A Scale of feet for the Altar according to Perspective.

The Scale of feet.

5 10 15 20 25 30 35 40 45 50 55 60 65 70 75 80 85 90 95 100

MBurghers ʃculp.

45. Michael Burghers, *The Orthography and Ichnography of Trinity College Chappel in Oxford*, revised version, c.1693.

Bathurst's design was initially turned over to Hawksmoor to look at, and that Wren or Hawksmoor then produced an agreed design that took better account of what he knew of the Chapel's site in the College.

The Hawksmoor design is more radical than it looks at first sight. He has devised a façade that is assertively symmetrical up to the level of the basement of the balustrade. The upper storey of the tower now appears more like a pavilion. An austerely corniced Doric portico marks a rectangular entrance into the court-yard, and is matched precisely at the left, albeit with a blank door to be inscribed in honour of the College's foundation (and perhaps recording Bathurst's efforts). A barely legible under-drawing shows that the arrangement of pilasters and arches originally continued across what was to become the left end bay with its Doric portico. Slivers of pilaster mark the juncture of the main window façade with the protruding end bays – in a sophisticated manner. The entrance to the Chapel has been matched on the left by a second door next to the end bay. The problem of the articulation of the balustrade with its fiddly pinnacles has been solved through the addition of pedestals, though the 'vases' that Wren mentions are only present on the tower in the form of flaming urns.

There may be an element of pipe-dreaming with respect to the revised elevation of the façade. Hawksmoor's scheme takes no notice of the abutting wing of the old Durham College courtyard. Moreover, Wren himself suspected that Bathurst's building was 'too far advanced to admit of any advice'. However the troublesome upper region above the main cornice was still open for revision, and was duly adjusted, and, as we will see, a change may have been made to the tower staircase in keeping with Wren's suggestion. It may well be that the present main cornice also adopts the profile proposed in one of Wren's two alternative designs. Whatever Wren sent in his deal box – whether it was identical to the Hawksmoor drawing or less radical – it could only have exercised a limited impact.

The final piece of visual evidence is a second, revised engraving by Burghers (fig. 45), which is more problematic than is at first evident. The copper plate for it survives in the College Archives (fig. 46). The main outlines have been taken over from the first print, duplicated by the mechanical means of transfer at which print-makers were adept, including tracing. The title and date on the cartouche remain the same, though the lettered key to the labelling of the parts has changed. But the engraving cannot itself date from 1691, since it reflects the Wren-

46. Michael Burghers, copper plate for *The Orthography and Ichnography of Trinity College Chappel in Oxford*, revised version.

inspired modifications from the spring of the following year. The year 1691 is retained, presumably, as the founding date, not the date of the design and engraving as such. We might then think that it was made in 1692 to trumpet the new design, but the engraving corresponds closely to the finished state of the Chapel, allowing for the tiny scale of some of the details.

The exterior is as executed, with the exception that the pilaster/pier arrangement between the windows is not carried over into the built design, as we have already noted. The more orthodox arrangement in the two engravings and Hawksmoor design simply remains out of step with what was already built. The statues on the tower in the engraving reflect the final arrangement, as do the urns or vases on the balustrade. Astronomy with her sphere is clearly identifiable on the right corner of the tower, with Medicine on the left. The plan shows the final complex geometry of Peisley's marble floor, and we have noted that his contract in November 1693 makes specific reference to 'the printed design'. The plan of the staircase in the tower eliminates the diagonal passage visible in the first engraving, presumably in response to Wren's doubts about its structural probity. The two putti over the centre of the oak panelling are depicted in a way that gives a good impression on such a tiny scale of their communicative glances and gestures. Two Evangelists are present on the cornice above the door in the screen – Matthew with his angel is identifiable on the left and Mark with his lion on the right – but they seem to be engaged more conventionally with writing their Gospels rather than looking excitedly at Christ in the ceiling. The winged figure on the left of the cornice over the altar holds a palm, while that on the right brandishes a wreath – thus supporting their identification as Victories rather than angels. Most notably, the ceiling is very much as executed. The paintings, now correctly oriented to make

47. Michael Burghers, *The Orthography and Ichnography of Trinity College Chappel in Oxford*, first version, detail of the proposed ceiling painting.

48. Michael Burghers, *The Orthography and Ichnography of Trinity College Chappel in Oxford*, revised version, detail of the actual ceiling painting.

sense for the spectator entering the Chapel, are recorded with a striking degree of attention to detail (figs 47, 48). Even the small shields running along the cornice are indicated.

Given the speed and complexity with which the interior of the Chapel must have developed towards its final form, and the *ad hoc* adjustments that would be inevitable as the painters, sculptors, craftsmen and builders worked rapidly alongside each other and under the patron's and Sykes's eyes, it is highly unlikely that there was a definitive overall design available for Burghers to copy in 1692. However, the print does seem to have been in existence in November 1693, when Peisley's contract for the marble floor specifically refers to it. By this time most of the design decisions must have been taken, with the most notable exception being the poses of the Evangelists. The print was probably commissioned by the College to promote late fundraising and as a commemorative image in anticipation of the triumphant culmination of Bathurst's campaign. I wonder if each benefactor received a copy as a thank-you. This second print survives in some numbers, including impressions on wove paper, which was only introduced in the mid-eighteenth century. Presumably the College ordered later reprintings from the copper plate, which is still in sound condition.

The architectural shell of the building, that is to say excluding all the interior woodwork, carving and painting, is amenable in design if sometimes ungrammatical in its details, as we have seen. As the first classical chapel in Oxford, it warrants attention. However, it would not in itself be regarded as one of the most important and individual works of the period. It is the interior – its intricate iconography and artistic power – that serves to endow 'our whole design' with the special qualities that lend it continued significance.

3 'CURIOUSLY PAINTED...
VERY FFINE CARVING'

The interior decoration of the Chapel – the painting, figure sculpture, relief
carving, plaster, wooden architecture and panelling – works as a brilliantly
integrated ensemble. It speaks of a team of busy executants working very
effectively together under the direction of someone who was in total control of
all aspects of its imagery and function. As we noted, the College accounts for
this period do not provide adequate answers about who was involved. In fact, the
names of the artists responsible are nowhere recorded. Peisley and Frogley, the
two names we do have, are not candidates for the sculpture and paintings.

In the case of the ceiling paintings, there is no great problem identifying the
author. The engraver, antiquarian and informative busy-body, George Vertue,
who made sure that he was well briefed about art in England, recorded in one
of his many notebooks, 'Trinity Coll. Chap. The Ceiling painted by Berchet', and
provided a biographical outline of the painter.[43] He tells us that Pierre (or Peter)
Berchet was born in France in 1659 and had been a pupil of Charles de La Fosse.
Berchet had worked twice in England before emigrating permanently in 1685.[44] He
was a Huguenot and the religious climate in France was threatening his livelihood.
His animated and accomplished French style was well received, though he was not
successful in the competition to win the commission to paint the dome of St Paul's.
The Trinity ceiling is his finest surviving work on a large scale.

From La Fosse, Berchet had learnt the Italian – above all the Venetian –
technique for narrating great religious and secular narratives on ceilings, using a
form of illusionism that allowed the actors to be visible coherently from below.
The solution is to paint the air-borne scene as if we are looking into the space
above us from an angle at or outside the lower margin of the picture. Thus in the
Trinity ceiling, as we have noted, we look up diagonally from the point at which we
enter the main body of the Chapel. The two largest angels vigorously anchor the
base of the composition, with inviting gestures and reverent glances. There are
echoing gestures and glances in the densely orchestrated figure group above. The
foreshortening of Christ's body is handled well as he rises into the golden glare of
heaven. The colours exhibit a Venetian warmth, and the strongly directional light
from the centre models the limbs of the figures with some vigour. Berchet has
particularly delighted in the back-light on the jolly putto above Christ. The painter's
handling of the oil medium is confident, fluent and free (fig. 49). Darkened varnish
and an accumulation of surface grime have veiled the full force of the colours and

muted the tonal range, but his painting still conveys an energetic sense of spiritual uplift and divine radiance. In the lateral panels of putti with the symbols of the Passion, Berchet is able to be more freewheeling in how he treats the bodies in space than in the vertical narrative of the ascent of Christ. The French-trained artist makes such ceiling painting look easy and natural, but we only need look at Robert Streater's laboured painting of *Truth Casting out Ignorance* in Wren's Sheldonian Theatre to appreciate that it is very difficult to orchestrate an aerial narrative with Berchet's facility.

The name of the other major participant in shaping the interior is also not in real doubt, in spite of the dearth of documents. Celia Fiennes described 'a very ffine Carving of thin white wood just Like that at Windsor it being the same hand'. The hand is that of Grinling Gibbons. Indeed, no one has seriously questioned that the wonderful limewood carving of angels and naturalistic motifs in the reredos shows Gibbons at his best. The Dutch-born sculptor has been rather typecast as a specialist in such things, but this is to misrepresent his career and certainly does not reflect his own self-image. He was a designer and maker of major monuments, altarpieces and church furnishings, creating substantial baroque ensembles of sculpture and architectural settings. He was also the creator of important free-standing statues, most notably the ambitious bronze statue of James II in Roman uniform, now standing in front of the National Gallery, and the gilded figure of Charles II in similar garb at the Royal Hospital Chelsea.

Born to an English merchant in Rotterdam, he trained as a sculptor in Holland, probably with one of the members of the highly successful Quellin family of carvers.[45] Having moved to England in the late 1660s, he enjoyed a steady rise, and by 1680 was described as the 'King's Carver', becoming the 'Master Sculptor and Carver in Wood to the Crown' in 1683. One of the grandest projects on which he worked was the sculpture for the Roman Catholic chapel commissioned by James II for Whitehall. In 1685 we learn that Gibbons and Quellan [Arnold Quellin] had been contracted 'to erect an Altar piece in his Ma[ts] new Chappell in Whitehall … with clean white marble, free from Vents, with pillastors of white, well veind marble, and Collums of purple Ranee, the Shafts of both to be in whole stones and the work adorned with Statues and other Sculptures according to a … designe … made … by S[r] Christopher Wren Knt.'[46] Later removed and dismantled because of its 'Popish' qualities, it only survives as fragments in Burnham Church in Somerset, including suave marble angels. Gibbons was to continue as a close and well-paid collaborator of Wren's, not least at St Paul's in the years immediately following the completion of Trinity Chapel.

A good idea of Gibbons's ambitions as a designer of grand structures can be gained from his unexecuted design for a noble monument to William and Mary

50. Grinling Gibbons, *Design for a monument to William and Mary*, ink on paper.

51. Grinling Gibbons, detail of left drop of reredos, showing dowel for securing the upper layer of carving.

overleaf
52. Grinling Gibbons, limewood carvings above the reredos.

(fig. 50).[47] Above a majestic array of columns, winged figures playing trumpets draw back the curtains of a canopy to disclose vivacious putti bearing a crown, palm and halo. Below the flying figures are the lion and unicorn, while Order of the Garter stars are placed beside reliefs of St George. The monarchs are gilded by a burst of miraculous light, and are flanked by the theological virtues: Hope, Justice, Prudence and Charity. Three female mourners convey their sadness at the departure of the King and Queen from our mortal realm. Although the rhetoric of the tomb design is different from that of Bathurst's Chapel, Gibbons's composition of architectural and sculptural motifs in this and other executed projects for tombs demonstrates that he was well capable of acting as the orchestrator of advanced baroque ensembles, and more specifically of conceiving the architecture of the screen and the altar wall in Trinity. As a prominent collector of and dealer in Continental paintings, he would also have been more than alert to the possibilities presented by the Franco-Italian style practised by Berchet.

That Gibbons put his own hand to the carvings around the altarpiece frame cannot be doubted. They are carved from limewood, which had been much used for virtuoso sculpture in Europe and which he energetically promoted in Britain. The complex plant motifs are built up from up to three layers of limewood with a miraculous fineness of undercutting. The layers are secured to each other by dowels (fig. 51). The various putti and 'cedar' screens are also readily recognisable as his work. He was especially good at chubby infants (figs 52, 53).

It is also reasonable to think that he was responsible for the larger figure sculptures, the two Victories and four Evangelists. However, if we look at them carefully, they seem to differ from his customary manner of carving. The draperies of the Evangelists, as they contort their bodies and wrench their faces heavenwards, exhibit an angular impetus that becomes a visual motif in its own right. Only here and there does the cloth cling to the figures, declaring the forms beneath. More often they surge in sharp-edged waves, abruptly changing direction and rising into pointed peaks. Sometimes, as on St Mark, they bunch into jagged crumples like screwed-up paper. The heads, hands and feet by contrast are naturalistic in a rather classicising mode.

A search for something similar amongst sculptors in Britain at this time has not yielded anything truly comparable. It is possible they are by one of the many foreign sculptors who were arriving in Britain to take advantage of the amount of work that was becoming available. Caius Cibber from Denmark, who as we have already noted was responsible for the statues on Wren's library for Trinity College, Cambridge, could turn his hand to draperies in baroque motion, but never in such

54. Grinling Gibbons, *St Luke*, viewed from below, showing the shallow nature of the sculpture.

53. Grinling Gibbons, detail of carved infants in left drop of reredos.

an angular mode. Cibber is a candidate for the carving of the female allegorical figures on the Chapel tower, but they are so deteriorated that stylistic analysis is all but impossible. For the Evangelists we might look to John Nost (Jan van Ost) from Belgium who acted as foreman to Gibbons's collaborator Arnold Quellin before the latter's death in 1686.[48] However, his fine memorial of 1692 to Sir Hugh Wyndham in St Nicholas's Parish Church, Silton is conspicuously more classical in the way it handles the draperies of Wyndham and his two wives. Amongst the native English sculptors, the most virtuoso master of semi-autonomous and agitated drapery was the pugnacious John Bushnell, who acquired an idiosyncratic and fully baroque manner from his early years wandering in Europe.[49] However, his drapery style is more overtly Italianate in manner. There is no sign that the erratic and litigious Bushnell was associated with Gibbons or worked in Oxford. Looking at the work of the numerous carvers active in Oxford during the Restoration, such as William Byrd, who worked on the Sheldonian Theatre, it is difficult to find anything that quite chimes with the fractured linear energy of the Chapel statues.

I think the explanation for the difficulty of finding precise parallels lies in their odd technical characteristics, the peculiarities that are not immediately apparent to the observer on the floor of the Chapel. They are carved in a juniper wood, that is to say Bermuda cedar, which is not a wood normally used for sculpture. They are, in spite of their apparent bulk, very shallow (fig. 54). The figures are in effect carved in high relief and are somewhat less than half a figure in depth. The attributes of the Evangelists, also carved in relief, are quite crudely 'patched in'. The rear planes of the sculptures are notably rough, and we can see that the consistency of the wood is hardly encouraging for a figure sculptor. Wood necessarily elicits a different response from the sculptor than stone and bronze, and each wood must be treated according to its own nature. The 'cedar' provided for the sculptor seems not to have lent itself to swinging curves and the classical 'wet-style' drapery that emphasises the figures' poses. Even the swags around the perforated panels on the screens, also in 'cedar', are more angular than we might normally expect. I think what we are seeing with the Evangelists, and in a less pronounced way with the Victories, is a very clever and adaptable response by Gibbons to a form of wood carving that he would not himself have chosen, all things being equal. He is indulging in very ingenious sleights of hand, creating an illusion of corporality in figures that are as insubstantial in their own way as the projected sculptures in his pen-and-wash drawings. Protruding heads, hands and feet, plus distracting folds of surging drapery, trick us into believing that there are bodies where none exist (fig. 55).

The sculptor of the Evangelists, whom I am taking to be Gibbons, must have conspired with Berchet in determining how the spatial ensemble would work. We have noted that the 1691 scheme as reflected in the engraving showed an Ascension-cum-Transfiguration on the ceiling. The subject of Berchet's painting is probably best described as *Christ in Glory*. The Ascension involved the disciples as witnesses: 'While they beheld, he was taken up; and a cloud received him out of their sight' (Acts 1:9). In paintings of the Ascension the disciples are invariably present as astonished witnesses. This is the case with the version of the painting recorded in

the first engraving, which also seems to allude to the Transfiguration (see fig. 47). Christ's Transfiguration was witnessed by three disciples: 'After six days Jesus taketh with him Peter, and James, and John his brother, and bringeth them up into a high mountain apart: and he was transfigured before them; and his face did shine as the sun, and his garments became white as the light' (Matthew 17: 1–3). We have seen that the radiance of divine light is a central theme in the Chapel. In the painting as executed by Berchet, there are no disciples within the pictorial field. Rather the witnesses, in the persons of two (or four) of the Evangelists are relocated on to the screen. As such they recall the disciples in the Transfiguration rather than the larger number present at the Ascension.

The idea of conducting a narrative across the space of an interior was introduced in sixteenth-century Italy and taken up in seventeenth-century France. La Fosse, Berchet's master, knew Italian examples first-hand, having spent some years in Rome and Venice. On his own account, La Fosse exercised his talents as an illusionistic painter in England when he was invited in 1689 by the Duke of Montagu to decorate his London house, where he completed wall and ceiling paintings in 1692.[50] Montagu House was demolished in the 1840s to make way for the building of the British Museum. The dynamic spatial composition by Berchet

56. Grinling Gibbons, *St John*, viewed from the east.

and Gibbons is ambitious, even by Continental standards, and very ambitious in British terms. The intensity of emotional interplay is remarkable (figs 55, 56). In the iconographical subtlety of the *Christ in Glory* we may suspect that the theological mind of Bathurst has been at work. If so, we can gain some insight into the kinds of collaboration that are necessary to achieve the levels of integration of form and content witnessed in Trinity Chapel.

In short, there is nothing surviving in Britain that is quite like the Chapel in terms of the sum of its parts, even if it remains indelibly English in the main disposition of its architecture and its functional arrangements. We can find comparisons for the architectural articulation, for Gibbons's sculpture, for the fine panelling, and even for the illusionistic ceiling. The closest parallel in England for the painting is Louis Laguerre's *Christ in Glory* on the ceiling in the chapel at Chatsworth, the decoration of which was underway at the same time as the Trinity project. Laguerre also worked on a large scale as an illusionist painter at Blenheim. However, none of the comparators combine painting and sculpture in as ingenious a manner as was accomplished by Berchet and Gibbons at Trinity. It may be that the destroyed Catholic chapel of James II in Whitehall rivalled its baroque integration, but the surviving evidence and fragments suggest not.

The founder of the College, Sir Thomas Pope, flourished in the reign of the Catholic Queen, Mary Tudor, and he was always uncomfortable with the radical aspects of Protestant dogma. We may imagine that he would have been happy with the spirit of the decorations in his college's new Chapel. The inlaid woodwork that stands in for an altarpiece would have puzzled him, and he may have been disconcerted by the 'modern' style of the architecture and decorations, but we may imagine that he would have readily acknowledged the spiritual import of Bathurst's creation.

I think, in conclusion, that we can justly identify Bathurst as the 'author' of the Chapel, as its *genius loci*. In fact he is still there; he was buried in the antechapel beneath a simple marble lozenge (fig. 57). He can be justly proud of what he called the Chapel's 'handsome perfection'. Samuel du Gard's praise was equally apt: 'For Strength and Beauty it is reckoned among the Chief Ornaments of the university'. This is as true now as it ever has been.

57. Burial marker of Ralph Bathurst in the antechapel.

APPENDIX
Seven Saints: The Windows of the Chapel
EMMA PERCY

58. John William Brown for J.B. Powell & Co., *Virgin Mary*.

Bathurst's magnificent new Chapel was designed with eight large windows of plain glass, and that was how it remained until the Victorian era. The first stained glass to be placed in the Chapel was a window paid for by public subscription in memory of Isaac Williams, who died in 1865. Made of Flemish glass and depicting the Crucifixion, it was placed in the antechapel over the entrance. Williams was a key figure in the Oxford Movement with its love of decoration and ritual. The decision to commemorate him in a stained-glass window was in keeping with a trend then prevalent in churches and chapels throughout the country. Plain glass windows were being replaced or embellished with stained glass, often as memorials. Many of the college chapels in Oxford that had no medieval glass began to acquire Victorian stained glass in this way.

Anticipating the piecemeal donation of further memorial windows, and concerned about how the resulting mixture of stained glass would affect the beauty of the building, the then Bursar, Henry G. Woods, decided to replace all the plain glass with a set of matching windows. In 1885 he devised a scheme for the seven remaining windows and ordered them from J.B. Powell & Co. of Whitechapel, one of the leading stained glass factories. The designer was John William Brown of Newcastle. They were a personal gift by Williams, which cost him a little over £1,000, in memory of his tenure as a Fellow.

The timing of this gift is interesting. Woods had been a Fellow of the College since 1865 and was considered a very dedicated member of the Fellowship. At this stage Fellows were not allowed to retain their fellowship if married, and by the late 1870s Woods had fallen in love with 'Daisy', Margaret Louisa Woods, daughter of Revd George Bradley, Dean of Westminster. In 1878 President Wayte retired and Woods stood for election, knowing that as President he could stay in the College and get married. However, the election of 1878 was disputed, and Woods's rival John Percival became the new President.

Woods resigned his fellowship and married Daisy, moving into Holywell Street. Under new statutes his fellowship was frozen but he was appointed Bursar and Tutor, retaining his involvement in the College but not as a Fellow. By the early 1880s Percival's frustrations in his role as President were becoming known and the fact that he might be thinking of resigning may have prompted Woods's generosity to the College.

The windows were given by Woods whilst Bursar, the order book listing his address as 28 Holywell Street. If he did indeed feel that such a generous gift might help his chances in the next election, Woods's hopes were soon fulfilled, since he was duly elected President in 1887, a year after the windows were installed. Whatever the exact reasons for his munificence, the Chapel benefited from his forestalling a mixed set of windows and instead providing a unified design that works well within the baroque Chapel.

The order book at J.B. Powell & Co. states 'own scheme' in the margins, and it seems that it was Woods himself who detailed what should go in the windows. The key to understanding this scheme are the two coats of arms in the central windows on either side, belonging respectively to Thomas Pope, founder of Trinity College, and Thomas Hatfield, Bishop of Durham from 1345 to 1381. Pope was the founder and original benefactor of Trinity College and here his arms are linked with Hatfield's. Bishop Hatfield did not found Durham College, but he was responsible for endowing the College through his will. The will provided for eight student monks from Durham to be known as 'Fellows' and eight secular students called 'pueri' or 'scholars'. Thus with his benefaction Durham College became not simply an Oxford home for Durham monks but a college for scholars.

In Woods's scheme the windows are intended to celebrate these two benefactors and to connect together the two colleges, making a particular point about the continuity of worship on the site. He cleverly brings something of the old chapel into the new. The original chapel, built in the 1400s and dedicated in January 1410, is described by John Aubrey in Herbert Blakiston's history of the College as having three bays with perpendicular windows and an east window, all containing stained glass:

> *Md that the windowes here were very good Gothique painting like those of New College, and I think better, in every columne a figure, e.g., St. Cuthbert, St. Leonard, St. Oswald, I have forgott the rest. 'Tis pitty they should be lost.... The glasse of these windows in the time of presbytery government were taken downe and now is there only plain glasse.*[51]

59. John William Brown for J.B. Powell & Co., *St Cuthbert*.

60. John William Brown for J.B. Powell & Co., *St Benedict*.

Aubrey also notes that there were two side altars, one dedicated to St Catherine and the other to Christ's deposition from the cross.

In devising a scheme that linked the old chapel with the new, Woods has clearly taken note of this description. For each window he chose a single figure of a saint, selecting those mentioned in Aubrey's account. Thus we have St Cuthbert, St Leonard, St Oswald and St Catherine, to whom a side altar had been dedicated. He added to these St Benedict, the Venerable Bede and St Mary, all with clear links to Durham and therefore to Durham College. As well as these single figures, Woods asked for three royal coats of arms and the coats of arms of Pope, Hatfield, the University and the Bishop of Winchester to be included, one in each of the seven windows.

Looking at the windows, Woods's scheme can be fully appreciated. On the south side there are four windows, each of them featuring a coat of arms at the

top. Moving from the altar, these are: the arms of Thomas Pope with his motto, *quod tacitum velis nemini dixeris* – what you wish kept secret, tell no one; the arms of Oxford University; the arms of Thomas Hatfield, Prior and Bishop of Durham; the arms of the Bishop of Winchester, the College visitor. Apart from the middle window, which contains the arms of Hatfield and Pope, each window has a small scene at the base. These depict the Annunciation, the Nativity and the Adoration of the Magi. The main feature of each window is a large single figure of a saint.

The window nearest the altar features the **Blessed Virgin Mary** (fig. 58). Mary is an obvious choice to include, being one of the dedicatees of the original grant of land from the nunnery of Godstow to the monastery at Durham for the building of a college in Oxford (the others being God the Father, St Cuthbert, and the Prior and convent of Durham). With Christ, Mary is the dedicatee of Durham Cathedral and would have been important to the early days of Trinity, which was founded as a Catholic house of learning under Queen Mary. Unusually, Mary stands alone with none of the standard iconographic symbols, though her blue cloak would probably be a strong enough clue to her identity even without the inscription.

Next to Mary, appropriately, is **St Cuthbert** (fig. 59). He is depicted as a bishop, and cradles Durham Cathedral in his arms. From what we know of Cuthbert's early life he was a shepherd turned soldier who then became a monk in the monastery of Melrose. He eventually became Prior of Melrose Abbey, and was known for his pastoral work and preaching across the rugged northern landscape. In 664 he was sent to be the Prior of Lindisfarne, Holy Island, to help the priory adapt to the new Roman ways following the Synod of Whitby. He is remembered both for his work as prior and his work in the wider community preaching and caring for the people. As he got older, Cuthbert increasingly longed to withdraw from the world, moving to one of the Farne Islands off the Northumberland coast to live as a hermit. He was not left in peace, though, as people constantly sought his advice, and in 684 he was elected Bishop of Lindisfarne. But his episcopacy was brief, ill health causing him to resign and spend his last weeks in the solitude he so desired.

Cuthbert was buried on Lindisfarne, and his grave became a place of pilgrimage. About 100 years later, constant raids by the Vikings made the priory unsafe for the monks, who set out to find a new home, taking Cuthbert's body with them. They settled first at Chester-le-Street before moving to a rocky peninsula in a loop of the River Wear which was to grow into the city of Durham. The great Norman cathedral was built to house Cuthbert's shrine, and he still lies buried behind the high altar.

The next window includes the figure of **St Benedict** (fig. 60). Benedict was born in central Italy around 480. He lived as a hermit in Subiaco and soon attracted a group of disciples, which led to the founding of some small monasteries. He moved to Monte Cassino where, as abbot, he wrote a rule for monks. The rule covered all aspects of a monk's daily life, providing for seven daily offices and setting out the manner of living together. The rule offered a balance between prayer, study and work and was so good that it became widely used in monasteries throughout Western Christendom. The Benedictine order grew out of the rule book. From the eighth to the twelfth century it was the predominant model of Western monasticism. The monastery at Durham adopted the Benedictine rule, and the first monks who studied on this site at Durham College would have continued to live according to it. The figure is dressed in a Benedictine habit and holds both rule book and quill.

In the antechapel we find a representation of the **Venerable Bede** (fig. 61). Bede's grave also lies in Durham Cathedral. Born in Northumbria in 670, he was sent to the monastery at Monkwearmouth as a young boy. In 682 or thereabouts he moved to the monastery at Jarrow and lived there as a monk for the rest of his life. He is remembered as a scholar and particularly as a historian; his best known work is *Historia ecclesiastica gentis Anglorum*, a history of England from the time of Caesar up to the book's completion in 729. He also wrote many commentaries and lives of the saints. Here he is depicted holding the *Historia* and dressed as a monk.

The north side of the Chapel has only three stained-glass windows because, when Woods designed the scheme, the window over the door was the Isaac Williams memorial window. This window was removed when the Chapel underwent renovation work in the 1960s. It still lies in storage as previous members of the Fellowship chose not to have it reinstated.

The three windows on the north side each have a royal coat of arms at the top. Looking from the altar they are the arms of: Philip and Mary 1554, marking the foundation of Trinity College; Queen Victoria 1885, marking the installation of the stained glass; King Edward III 1339. It has been hard to establish why this last date is given, but it is the date listed in the order book. One might assume that it marked the founding of Durham College, but accounts suggest that it was established earlier. Hatfield's endowment was not given until after his death in 1381, though he first made arrangements in 1379. The significance of the date 1339 therefore remains a mystery. Two of the windows have small subjects: Christ being taken from the cross and the empty tomb.

Nearest the altar we find the figure of **St Catherine of Alexandria** (fig. 62). Aubrey notes that there was an altar to Catherine in the first chapel. She is a legendary figure who became particularly popular in the Middle Ages when many chapels and churches were dedicated to her, the ancient monastery on Mount Sinai being renamed in her honour. The legend tells of a young woman who was taken from Alexandria during the persecution of the Christian church by Emperor Maxentius in the early fourth century. She was put to dispute with many pagan philosophers and converted many of them to Christianity and martyrdom. She herself was subjected to 'martyrdom' on a spiked wheel, but the wheel was miraculously destroyed and she was then beheaded. Catherine's scholarly debating meant that she became the patron saint of scholars and librarians, which is perhaps why she was included in the old chapel and in this one. She stands with her wheel, though the angle makes it difficult to identify.

Next to Catherine is **St Oswald, King of Northumbria** (fig. 63). Oswald had taken refuge in the monastery on the isle of Iona after his father's death while the kingdom was ruled by the ruthless tyrant Cadwallon. Having been baptised on Iona, he set out to win back his kingdom. Legend has him setting up a wooden

61. John William Brown for J.B. Powell & Co., *Venerable Bede*.

62. John William Brown for J.B. Powell & Co., *St Catherine of Alexandria*.

63. John William Brown for J.B. Powell & Co., *St Oswald, King of Northumbria.*

64. John William Brown for J.B. Powell & Co., *St Leonard.*

cross on the battlefield and encouraging his soldiers to pray with him before winning a great victory against Cadwallon in 633. He then became King of Northumbria, his influence stretching across all of Britain.

Wishing to convert the people of his kingdom to Christianity, he sent to Iona for a missionary. The first one found it hard going and went home. The second was Aidan, who founded the monastery on Lindisfarne not far from Oswald's main castle at Bamburgh. With Oswald's support, he spread the Christian faith across Northumbria. Oswald was killed in battle in 642 and dismembered. His head was taken to Lindisfarne, and when the monks left the isle it was placed in Cuthbert's tomb and is reputedly still there.

The last window contains the figure of **St Leonard** (fig. 64). Leonard was one of the saints Aubrey lists as being in the original chapel windows, and this presumably is why he is here, since there is no obvious connection between Leonard and Durham. Again he was an extremely popular medieval saint. A sixth-century French hermit who turned down the chance to be a bishop, legend says that he successfully petitioned King Clovis to free many prisoners. He is also supposed to have assisted Queen Clothilde in her labour, thus making him patron saint of prisoners and childbearing women and thus a somewhat unlikely saint for Trinity College!

The St Oswald window includes two small coats of arms. One belongs to Henry Woods, a fitting reminder of his generous donation of the windows, while the other interestingly is that of the then President, John Percival. A small note in the order book says that Mrs Percival was to pay for this.

The scheme devised by Woods has endowed Trinity Chapel with a coherent set of windows that celebrate the connection between the former Durham College and Trinity. The saints he chose provide a link with the old chapel and former college, and these are surrounded by Renaissance-style decorations designed to look well within the baroque masterpiece of Trinity College Chapel. The windows remind us of our benefactors and our history, as well as having prevented a piece-meal donation of glass that may have detracted from the order and beauty of the Chapel. Although figurative glass windows were not part of Bathurst's original conception, the present stained glass is nicely integrated into the overall appearance of the Chapel and has become an accepted part of its remarkably integrated effect.

NOTES

1 A literal transcription of Celia Fiennes's travel accounts can be found at http://www.visionofbritain.org.uk/text/chap_page.jsp?t_id=Fiennes&c_id=8. I have corrected the transcription of 'Lord Oxford' to 'Lord Orfford' for the reason explained below, p.18. All quotations from Fiennes's account are taken from this source.

2 Arthur McGregor, 'The Day the Tsar Came', *The Ashmolean*, no. 44 (Spring 2003), pp. 8–9.

3 The standard biography remains Thomas Warton, *The Life and Literary Remains of Ralph Bathurst, MD*, London, 1761. For Bathurst in the College, see Clare Hopkins, *Trinity: 450 Years of an Oxford College Community*, Oxford, 2005, chapter 6. For his philosophical stance and experimental science, see Jan Guy, 'Leading a Double Life: Ralph Bathurst (1620–1704): Physician-physiologist and Cleric', *Journal of Medical Biography*, 2006, pp. 17–22. For the history of the College and an account of Durham College, its predecessor, see also H. E. Salter and Mary D. Lobel, eds, 'Trinity College', in *A History of the County of Oxford: Volume 3: The University of Oxford*, London, 1954, pp. 238–51 (http://www.british-history.ac.uk/report.aspx?compid=63885, accessed 13 September 2013).

4 See the letter from Boyle to Bathurst (Trinity College Archives, Fellows 2/1/1). The lectures were not to appear in print until they were included in Warton's biography in 1761.

5 Hopkins, *Trinity*, pp. 9–15.

6 For biographies of Cibber and other British sculptors of this period, see the remarkable compilation by Ingrid Roscoe, with Emma Hardy and M. G. Sullivan, *A Biographical Dictionary of Sculptors in Britain, 1660–1851*, London, 2009.

7 Warton, *Life of Bathurst*, p. xxiii.

8 Dinah Birch, 'The Big Picture', *Trinity College Report*, 2001, pp. 73–6.

9 Trinity College Archive (hereafter 'TCA'), Misc. Vol. I, f. 90/145.

10 TCA Misc I, 90/146.

11 TCA Misc. I, 94d/164.

12 TCA Misc. I, 95/166.

13 TCA Misc. I, 94/158.

14 Ibid.

15 TCA Misc. I, 78d/121.

16 All Souls, I.72, I.69, I.68, I.71 and IV.66. For the drawings in All Souls, see the excellent catalogue by Anthony Geraghty, *The Architectural Drawings of Sir Christopher Wren at All Souls College, Oxford: A Complete Catalogue*, London, 2007, pp. 24–6.

17 TCA Misc. I, 82/126.

18 TCA Misc. I, 79/123.

19 TCA Misc. I, 83/128.

20 For a fuller account of the fundraising for the new residence and Bathurst's other improvements to the College buildings, see Hopkins, *Trinity*, pp.129–33.

21 TCA Misc. I, 84d/141.

22 TCA Misc. I, 89/142.

23 Geoffrey Tyack, *Modern Architecture in an Oxford College: St John's College, 1945–2005*, Oxford, 2005, Appendix I. For the Peisleys, see Roscoe, *Dictionary of Sculptors*, pp. 968–9, and Howard Colvin, *A Biographical Dictionary of British Architects 1600–1840*, rev edn, New Haven and London, 1995, pp.746–7.

24 Roscoe, *Dictionary of Sculptors*, pp. 968–9 and Colvin, *Dictionary of British Architects*, p. 746.

25 Colvin, *Dictionary of British Architects*, pp. 576–7.

26 TCA Misc. I, 89/143.

27 Anthony Wood, *The Life and Times of Anthony Wood 1632–1695, Described by Himself*, ed. Andrew Clark, 4 vols, Oxford, 1891–5, vol. 3, p. 364.

28 TCA Misc. I, 89/144.

29 TCA Misc. I, 92d/153.

30 Warton, *Life of Bathurst*, pp. 69–70.

31 TCA Misc. I, 94/159.

32 TCA Misc. I, 95/168.

33 TCA Misc. I, 95d/169.

34 Hopkins, *Trinity*, p. 157.

35 TCA Misc. I, 100/176, Benefactors' Book, 2, 8.

36 TCA Misc. I, 99/173.

37 TCA Misc. I, 99/174.

38 TCA Charters F/I/I.

39 TCA Misc. I, 99/175.

40 The English edition of 1824 is available at http://archive.org/details/elementsofcivila00aldrrich

41 Giles Worsley, ed., *The Role of the Amateur Architect*, London, 1994, especially Howard Colvin, 'What we mean by amateur', pp. 4–6. Colvin records eighty amateur architects between 1680 and 1820, of whom eight were in holy orders.

42 All Souls, II, 103, Geraghty, *Architectural Drawings of Wren*, p. 42, where it is correctly attributed to Hawksmoor.

43 George Vertue, 'Notebooks', *The Walpole Society*, XVIII (1929–30), p. 87.

44 Kathryn Barron, 'Berchet, Peter (1659–1720)', in *Oxford Dictionary of National Biography*, Oxford, 2004 (http://ezproxy.ouls.ox.ac.uk:2117/view/article/2185, accessed 4 February 2009).

45 Roscoe, *Dictionary of Sculptors*, pp. 511–9 provides an essential source for Gibbons and a complete list of known works. For Gibbons's career and sculpture, see David Green, *Grinling Gibbons: His Work as a Carver and Statuary 1648–1721*, London, 1964; Geoffrey Beard, *The Work of Grinling Gibbons*, Chicago, 1990; and David Esterly, *Grinling Gibbons and the Art of Carving*, London, 1998 (not least for Esterly's notable insights into Gibbons's wood-carving techniques).

46 See Montagu Cox and Philip Norman eds, *Survey of London*, XIII, 1930, chapter 3, 'The Roman Catholic Chapel' (http://www.british-history.ac.uk/report.aspx?compid=67776#s24, accessed 13 September 2013).

47 London, British Museum, 1881,0611.164.

48 Roscoe, *Dictionary of Sculptors*, pp. 913–6.

49 Ibid., pp. 174–6.

50 An 1845 watercolour in the British Museum by George Scharf shows the grand paintings in the staircase with the large illusionist ceiling (1862,0614.631). See: http://tinyurl.com/ScharfBM, accessed 13 September 2013.

51 John Aubrey, quoted by Herbert E. D. Blakiston, *Trinity College*, London, 1898, pp. 21, 22.

INDEX

Page numbers in **bold** refer to illustrations